The Mark of Cain

The Mark of Cain

Studies in Literature and Theology

by

STUART B. BABBAGE

WILLIAM B. EERDMANS PUBLISHING COMPANY
GRAND RAPIDS, MICHIGAN

Acknowledgment is hereby made of permission to quote from certain copyrighted material as follows: To the Public Trustee and The Society of Authors for quotations from *Saint Joan, John Bull's Other Island,* and *Major Barbara,* all by Bernard Shaw; to Faber and Faber Ltd. for quotations from *The Recovery of Belief* by C. E. M. Joad; to Harcourt, Brace and World, Inc. and Brandt & Brandt for quotations from *Down and Out in Paris and London* by George Orwell; to the Macmillan Company for quotations from *Collected Poems* by John Masefield (copyright 1912 by The Macmillan Company, renewed 1940 by John Masefield; reprinted with the permission of The Macmillan Company); to The Society of Authors and Dr. John Masefield O.M. for quotations from "The Everlasting Mercy"; to T. & T. Clark for quotations from "Significant Modern Writers: Franz Kafka" by W. B. J. Martin, *Expository Times,* July 1960; to The Viking Press, Inc. for quotations from *A Portrait of the Artist as a Young Man* by James Joyce (copyright 1916 by B. W. Huebsch, 1944 by Nora Joyce; reprinted by permission of The Viking Press, Inc.); to the Executors of the James Joyce Estate and to Jonathan Cape Limited for quotations from *the Essential James Joyce;* to the Viking Press, Inc. for quotations from *Death of a Salesman* by Arthur Miller (copyright © 1949 by Arthur Miller; reprinted by permission of The Viking Press, Inc.); to Random House, Inc. and Alfred A. Knopf, Inc. for quotations from *No Exit and Three Other Plays* by Jean-Paul Sartre, translated by Stuart Gilbert (copyright 1946 by Stuart Gilbert; reprinted by permission of Alfred A. Knopf, Inc.), and for quotations from *The Fall* by Albert Camus, translated by Justin O'Brien (© copyright 1956 by Alfred A. Knopf, Inc.; reprinted by permission); to Harcourt, Brace & World, Inc. for quotations from "The Hollow Men" by T. S. Eliot (*The Complete Poems and Plays*), and for quotations from *Murder in the Cathedral* by T. S. Eliot, (copyright, 1935, by Harcourt, Brace & World, Inc., copyright, 1963, by T. S. Eliot, reprinted by permission of the publishers), and for quotations from *The Family Reunion* (copyright, 1939, by T. S. Eliot, reprinted by permission of Harcourt, Brace & World, Inc.), and for quotations from *The Cocktail Party* (copyright, 1950, by T. S. Eliot, reprinted by permission of Harcourt, Brace & World, Inc.).

To

VERONICA, MALCOLM, CHRISTOPHER AND TIMOTHY

Contents

Introduction

Samuel Hamilton, in John Steinbeck's novel *East of Eden*, relates: "Two stories have haunted us and followed us from our beginning, the story of original sin and the story of Cain and Abel. And I don't understand either of them."[1] It is these stories which provide the pattern for Steinbeck's exploration of the mystery of inherited guilt, of recurrent evil, first in the unhappy lives of Adam and his brother Charles, and then in the lives of Adam's twins, Caleb and Aron. Lee, the faithful Chinese servant, who has the instincts of a philosopher, insists that the curse of guilt can be lifted. He tells them that, in the biblical narrative, when God speaks to Cain, He uses the Hebrew word *timshel*. This word, Lee explains, carries with it, if not the promise, at least the possibility of victory: "Thou *mayest* triumph over sin." The conclusion of the novel, nakedly expressed, is: " *'Thou mayest, Thou mayest!'* What glory!"[2]

Adam Trask arrives with his wife Cathy in Salinas Valley in the hope of establishing a new and happy home. Adam looks forward to creating an Eden, to which, he says, his name

---

[1] *East of Eden* (Viking, New York, 1952), p. 266.
[2] *Ibid.*, pp. 308-9.

9

entitles him. But Cathy is no Eve: after the birth of the twins, she viciously wounds her husband and departs. Adam reverts to a still darker existence. With Samuel Hamilton's help he begins to recover his will to live only to recognize the awful truth that his two sons are repeating and recapitulating, within their own experience, the pattern of rivalry and conflict which had been responsible for the destruction of his own boyhood home.

Robert Browning insists that it is possible to understand the problem of human perversity and sin only from the perspective of faith.

> 'Tis faith that launched point-blank her dart
> At the head of a lie — taught Original Sin,
> The corruption of Man's Heart.[3]

Sin, he implies, is too radical a problem, too deep-seated, to be solved by simple exhortations of a helpful kind. To the man who knows the depths of his own depravity the words "Thou mayest" are not a glorious possibility but a cruel mockery and a tantalizing jest.

Steinbeck has little understanding of the dimensions of saving faith, but he is able to explore, with extraordinary penetration, the destructive ramifications of sin. He takes as a basis for his analysis the ancient story of Cain and Abel, with its account of fratricidal strife and bitter alienation:

> Now Adam knew Eve his wife, and she conceived and bore Cain, saying, "I have gotten a man with the help of the Lord." And again, she bore his brother Abel. Now Abel was a keeper of sheep, and Cain a tiller of the ground. In the course of time Cain brought to the Lord an offering of the fruit of the ground, and Abel brought of the firstlings of his flock and of their fat portions. And the Lord had regard for Abel and his offering, but for Cain and his offering he had no regard. So Cain was very angry, and his countenance fell. The Lord said to Cain, "Why are you angry, and why has your countenance fallen? If you do well, will you not be accepted? And if you do not do well, sin is couching at the door; its desire is for you, but you must master it."

3 "Gold Hair."

Cain said to Abel his brother, "Let us go out to the field."
And when they were in the field, Cain rose up against his
brother Abel, and killed him. Then the Lord said to Cain,
"Where is Abel your brother?" He said, "I do not know;
am I my brother's keeper?" And the Lord said, "What have
you done? The voice of your brother's blood is crying to
me from the ground. And now you are cursed from the
ground, which has opened its mouth to receive your brother's
blood from your hand. When you till the ground, it shall no
longer yield to you its strength; you shall be a fugitive and
a wanderer on the earth." Cain said to the Lord, "My
punishment is greater than I can bear. Behold, thou hast
driven me this day away from the ground; and from thy face
I shall be hidden; and I shall be a fugitive and a wanderer
on the earth, and whoever finds me will slay me." Then
the Lord said to him, "Not so! If any one slays Cain,
vengeance shall be taken on him sevenfold." And the Lord
put a mark on Cain, lest any who came upon him should kill
him.
Then Cain went away from the presence of the Lord, and
dwelt in the land of Nod, east of Eden (Genesis 4:1-16).

It is a record of the first birth and the first murder. Adam
knows his wife in the deep personal intimacy of the sexual
relationship. By the mysterious metamorphosis of nature, Eve
becomes the mother of a son. With astonished joy she ex-
claims: "I have gotten a man." She calls him Cain. Another
son is born (possibly a twin), and she calls him Abel. As
Cain's name signifies accomplishment and achievement, so
Abel's name signifies decay and death. (In popular etymology,
abel means "a breath"; symbolically, it refers to that which
is transitory and fades away). The boys' names testify to the
fact that all human achievements are marked by mortality, and
that, in the midst of life, we are in death.

The deep tragedies of life, however, are associated, not with
its fleeting impermanence, but with man's inhumanity to man.
The measure of man's malice and malignity is the fact that the
closest relationships of life — the relationships of blood — are
not exempt from desecration and outrage. Cain's hate, signif-
icantly enough, finds its focus in a matter 'concerning religion.
So often in the history of the world man's highest activity —
the activity of worship — has been used as an excuse for the

perpetration of the most atrocious crimes. There is no hate like the ferocity of religious hate: "Pharisaic fury," comments Luther bluntly, "is a perfectly diabolical fury."[4] "To be furious in religion," William Penn insists, "is to be irreligiously religious."

The brothers, in the biblical story, bring their respective offerings to the Lord: Abel's offering is accepted and Cain's is rejected. The writer of the Epistle to the Hebrews adds this word of explanation: "By faith Abel offered to God a more acceptable sacrifice than Cain, through which he received approval as righteous, God bearing witness by accepting his gifts" (11:4). Abel had a right disposition; he was therefore approved as righteous. Cain's motives were not pure; consequently, his offering was rejected. Luther offers these reflections:

> Cain thought, indeed was confident, that his offering could not fail to please God far better than that of his brother. For thus he reasoned: I am the elder son, to me pertains the priestly service to God, and authority: moreover I bring the best offering. Therefore God will look upon my gift and be more pleased with it than with my brother Abel's. Abel on the other hand thought: I am the least, he is the best, he has the advantage over me and has brought the better sacrifice; therefore God must look upon my offering in pure grace.[5]

Cain's deep resentment expressed itself not only in sullen anger against God but also in bitter envy of his brother.

In the biblical narrative, God seeks to reason with Cain. "If you do well," God says, "will you not be accepted?" "If you do not well," He patiently explains, "sin is couching at the door; its desire is for you, but you must master it." So the Apostle Peter uses the same vivid and expressive simile to describe the activities of the devil — the simile of a devouring animal ready to spring: "Your adversary the devil prowls around like a roaring lion, seeking some one to devour" (1 Peter 5:8). Cain, however, refuses to own his sin, let alone to master it. Oblivious of the danger he is in, he recklessly in-

---

[4] Quoted, Wilhelm Vischer, *The Witness of the Old Testament to Christ,* translated by A. B. Crabtree (Lutterworth, London, 1949), p. 70.
[5] *Ibid.,* p. 71.

vites temptation by persuading his brother to go with him into the field when his heart is full of hate and murder. "Desire, when it has conceived, gives birth to sin," James observes, "and sin, when it is full grown, brings forth death" (1:15). The anticipated consequences follow: "When they were in the field, Cain rose up against his brother Abel, and killed him."

Cain is immediately aware of the accusing voice of God: "Where is Abel your brother?" Cain seeks to evade God's question by sullen denial: "I do not know: am I my brother's keeper?" To be human involves the acceptance of responsibility ("None of us," the Apostle Paul insists, "lives to himself" [Rom. 14:7]); by denying responsibility Cain denies his fitness to share in the life of the community. God is not deceived by Cain's mendacious denial: He compels him to face his guilt. "What have you done?" He asks. "The voice of your brother's blood is crying to me from the ground." God reminds Cain that He is the avenger of every act of injustice. Judgment is pronounced: the very ground is cursed (for the consequences of sin are always cosmic), and Cain is doomed to be a fugitive and a wanderer on the earth. His punishment means exclusion from the presence of God ("the hideous fall," says Luther, "from heaven to hell"[6]). Cain cries out: "My punishment is greater than I can bear!" Cain knows that God's face is turned away from him, and he fears that, being deserted by God, others will seek to kill him. In abject self-pity he sobs: "Whoever finds me will slay me."

God answers Cain's despairing cry with graciousness. He places a mark upon Cain to protect him from the further consequences of his own misdeeds. In His sovereign mercy God proclaims that He is not only the avenger and protector of the innocent victim but also the defender of the guilty murderer. He promises that He will restrain and set limits to the unbridled wickedness of men, thereby enabling Cain to live. In spite of his heinous crime, God places on him the mark of His ownership and possession. "The sign of Cain," says Wilhelm Vischer, "is at once a stigma and a sign of protection: anyone bearing it is publicly branded by God as a

---

[6] Quoted, W. Vischer, *op. cit.,* p. 73.

murderer of his brother; at the same time he is, by the same sign, protected as God's inviolable possession."[7]

We are all, as sinners, sons of Adam and brothers of Cain, and we bear his mark.   "We are all cruel," says Dostoevsky; "we are all monsters, we all make men weep — and mothers — and babes at the breast. . . ."[8]   We are all implicated and involved, "we are all estranged," says the Apostle Paul, "and hostile in mind, doing evil deeds" (Colossians 1:21).

"The supreme problem of the world," P. T. Forsyth insists, "is its sin.   Its one need is to be forgiven."[9]

It is not surprising that the themes of guilt and purgation continually recur in the literature of the world.   A single example from T. S. Eliot's early verse play, *The Family Reunion,* will suffice.   Harry, who has returned to the ancestral home for his mother's birthday, is weighed down with an insupportable burden of guilt.   He confesses that, one night, in mid-Atlantic, he pushed his wife overboard.   Since that night he has felt isolated on an island of guilt.   He speaks of "the partial anaesthesia of suffering without feeling"; the

> . . . *partial observation of one's own automatism*
> *While the slow stain sinks deeper through the skin*
> *Tainting the flesh and discolouring the bone —*

this, he says, is what matters, this is the inescapable reality.[10] "One thinks to escape," he says, "by violence, but one is still alone in an overcrowded desert, jostled by ghosts."   "It goes a good deal deeper," he explains, "than what people call their conscience"; it is something more awful than that: "it is the cancer that eats away the self."[11]   It is something far deeper than the bitterness of remorse, the awareness of being alone in one's guilt: "It's not being alone that is the horror," he bitterly explains; "what matters is the filthiness."   "I can clean

[7] *Op. cit.,* p. 75.

[8] *The Brothers Karamazov,* translated by Constance Garnett (Modern Library, New York, n.d.), p. 640.

[9] *Positive Preaching and the Modern Mind* (Hodder & Stoughton, London, n.d.), p. 333.

[10] *The Complete Poems and Plays,* 1909-1950 (Harcourt, Brace, New York, 1952), p. 235.

[11] *Ibid.,* p. 236.

my skin, purify my life, void my mind, but always there is the filthiness, that lies a little deeper. . . ."[12] "I know there is only one way out of defilement," he says, the road "which leads in the end to reconciliation."[13] For too long, he confesses, he has been vainly seeking to evade facing the implications of his guilt.

> . . . *All this year,*
> *This last year, I have been in flight*
> *But always in ignorance of invisible pursuers.*
> *Now I know that all my life has been a flight*
> *And phantoms fed upon me while I fled. Now I know*
> *That the last apparent refuge, the safe shelter,*
> *That is where one meets them.*[14]

He is now willing to admit his guilt, and, as a result, "on the other side of despair," he meets God. He discovers that the price of reconciliation (as for every penitent man who bears the mark of Cain) is

> *A stony sanctuary and a primitive altar,*
> *The heat of the sun and the icy vigil,*
> *A care over lives of humble people,*
> *The lesson of ignorance. . . .*[15]

T. S. Eliot's play ends liturgically with the recitation of a kind of litany as candles are extinguished one by one.

> *A curse is a power*
> *Not subject to reason*
> *Each curse has its course*
> *Its own way of expiation*
> > *Follow follow*

> *Not in the day time*
> *And in the hither world*
> *Where we know what we are doing*
> *There is not its operation*
> > *Follow follow*

[12] *Ibid.*, p. 269.
[13] *Ibid.*, p. 279.
[14] *Ibid.*, p. 280.
[15] *Ibid.*, p. 281.

But in the night time
And in the nether world
Where the meshes we have woven
Bind us to each other
              Follow follow

A curse is written
On the under side of things
Behind the smiling mirror
And behind the smiling moon
              Follow follow

This way the pilgrimage
Of expiation
Round and round the circle
Completing the charm
So the knot be unknotted
The cross be uncrossed
The crooked be made straight
And the curse be ended
By intercession
By pilgrimage. . . .[16]

[16] *Ibid.*, pp. 292-3.

The End of Innocence

or

the inveteracy of evil

For from within, out of the heart of man, come evil thoughts, fornication, theft, murder, adultery, coveting, wickedness, deceit, licentiousness, envy, slander, pride, foolishness. All these evil things come from within, and they defile a man (Mark 7:21-23).

Speaking of his long sojourn in the wilderness of agnosticism, C. E. M. Joad says:

It is because we rejected the doctrine of original sin that we on the Left were always being disappointed; disappointed by the refusal of people to be reasonable, by the subservience of intellect to emotion, by the failure of true Socialism to arrive, by the behaviour of nations and politicians, by the masses' preference for Hollywood to Shakespeare and for Mr. Sinatra to Beethoven; above all, by the recurrent fact of war.[1]

At church and Sunday school he had been taught that man is born in sin and that the heart of man is desperately wicked. These truths had been further enforced by the liturgy of the Church.

[1] *The Recovery of Belief* (Faber, London, 1952), p. 82.

The Confession told me that I had 'left undone those things which' I 'ought to have done', that there was 'no health' in me and that I was a 'miserable offender'. This view of me was further insisted on in the Communion Service in which I was led to 'acknowledge and bewail' my 'manifold sins and wickedness, which' I 'from time to time most grieviously' had 'committed, by thought, word and deed against' God's 'divine Majesty, provoking most justly' His 'wrath and indignation against' me.

The Collects reinforced the lesson, pointing out that I had no power of myself to help myself, and adding that without God 'the frailty of man . . . cannot but fall'. For this reason I was encouraged to pray earnestly for God's help. 'O God,' I prayed, 'because through the weakness of' my 'mortal nature' I 'can do no good thing without Thee, grant' me 'the help of Thy grace' — being assured that, if I prayed earnestly enough and earnestly endeavoured to live the kind of life that deserved it, God's grace would in fact be vouchsafed to me.[2]

The intellectual climate of the world in which he grew up, however, was antagonistic to these views. As a consequence, he discarded them. Instead, he embraced what he calls a "rational-optimist philosophy." Buttressed by the spectacular achievements of science, he came to believe not only in "the infinite malleability" of man, but also in "the infinite perfectibility of man."

It was the war which shattered these beliefs: "for the first time in my life," he relates, "the existence of God in the world made its impact upon me as a positive and obtrusive fact." As a result, he came to see that "evil is endemic in man, [and] that the Christian doctrine of original sin expresses a deep and essential insight into human nature."

In the sunny optimism of the late nineteenth century, it was easy for Joad and others of his generation to forget the truth about man's deep depravity, in the confidence that every day, in every way, man was getting better and better.

Dostoevsky knew better. He knew that within every man, even enlightened man, there is a strange streak of perversity, a strain of stubborn irrationality, an impulse of destructiveness.

[2] *Ibid.,* p. 47.

"Why does it happen," he enquires, "that at the very, yes, at the very moment when I am most capable of feeling every refinement of all that is 'good and beautiful,' as they used to say at one time, it would, as though of design, happen to me not only to feel but to do such ugly things. . . ." Dostoevsky is scornful of those who subscribe, in simple naïveté, to the belief that man is rational and good. "Man likes to make roads and to create, that is a fact beyond dispute. But why," he demands, "has he such a passionate love for destruction and chaos also. Tell me that!" The tragic truth is that educated man, even enlightened man, has a passion to destroy.

> Oh, tell me, who was it first announced, who was it first proclaimed, that man only does nasty things because he does not know his own interests; and that if he were enlightened, if his eyes were opened to his real normal interests, man would at once cease to do nasty things, would at once become good and noble because, being enlightened and understanding his real advantage, he would see his own advantage in the good and nothing else, and we all know that not one man can, consciously, act against his own interests, consequently, so to say, through necessity, he would begin doing good? Oh, the babe! Oh, the pure innocent child! Why, in the first place, when in all these thousands of years has there been a time when man has acted only from his own interest? What is to be done with the millions of facts that bear witness that men, consciously, that is fully understanding their real interests, have left them in the background and have rushed headlong on another path, to meet peril and danger, compelled to this course by nobody and by nothing, but, as it were, simply disliking the beaten track, and have obstinately, wilfully, struck out another difficult, absurd way, seeking it almost in the darkness?[3]

Thus, Dostoevsky says, in *Notes from Underground,* a man will often, without rhyme or reason, do things which are irrational and absurd.

> A man will talk to you with excitement and passion of the true normal interests of man; with irony he will upbraid the shortsighted fools who do not understand their own inter-

---

3 Walter Kaufmann, ed., *Existentialism from Dostoevsky to Sartre* (Meridian Books, New York, 1956), p. 67.

ests, nor the true significance of virtue; and, within a quarter
of an hour, without any sudden outside provocation, but
simply through something inside him which is stronger than
all his interests, he will go off on quite a different task —
that is, act in direct opposition to what he has just been
saying about himself, in opposition to the laws of reasons,
in opposition to his own advantage, in fact in opposition to
everything. . . .[4]

And, reflecting on the Crystal Palace which was erected in
London in 1851 to celebrate the Great Exhibition of Science,
he challenges the pretense of this venture, pointing out that it
is all very well to boast of building a "Palace of Crystal," but
asking where the guarantee is that someone will not be tempted
to smash it. With uncanny clairvoyance Dostoevsky forsees
that totalitarian tyrannies will arise dedicated to destruction.
(The Crystal Palace did not fall a victim to totalitarian tyranny,
but to an accidental fire. This fact, however, does not negate
Dostoevsky's argument.)

I, for instance, would not be in the least surprised if all of a
sudden, *a propos* of nothing, in the midst of general prosperity a gentleman with an ignoble, or rather with a re-
actionary and ironical, countenance were to arise and,
putting his arms akimbo, say to us all: 'I say, gentlemen,
hadn't we better kick over the whole show and scatter
rationalism to the winds, simply to send these logarithms to
the devil, and to enable us to live once more at our own
sweet foolish will!' That again would not matter, but what
is annoying is that he would be sure to find followers — such
is the nature of man.[5]

"Man," he emphasizes, "everywhere and at all times, whoever
he may be, has preferred to act as he chose and not in the
least as his reason and advantage dictated." That is the
depressing testimony of experience. Man's "worst defect,"
he solemnly repeats, "is perpetual moral obliquity."

Dostoevsky, however, was the voice of one crying in the
wilderness of nineteenth-century liberalism. That is why the
Western democracies were disconcerted by and unprepared

[4] *Ibid.,* p. 68.
[5] *Ibid.,* p. 71.

for the recrudescence of evil in the terrifying rise of "the Beast from the Abyss."

The Victorians prided themselves on their moral and technical achievements. Swinburne was moved to sing: "Glory to Man in the highest! for Man is the master of things."[6] John Addington Symonds echoed the same confidence:

> *These things shall be! A loftier race*
> *Than e'er the world hath known, shall rise*
> *With flame of freedom in their souls*
> *And light of science in their eyes.*
>
> *They shall be gentle, brave and strong,*
> *To spill no drop of blood, but dare*
> *All that may plant man's lordship firm*
> *On earth and fire and sea and air.*
>
> *New arts shall bloom of loftier world,*
> *And mightier music thrill the skies,*
> *And every life shall be a song,*
> *When all the earth is paradise.*[7]

The future, it appeared, was bright with promise. H. G. Wells was an apostle of this belief. He wrote:

> Can we doubt that presently our race will more than realise our boldest imaginations, that it will achieve unity and peace, that it will live, the children of our blood will live, in a world made more splendid and lovely than any palace or garden that we know, going on from strength to strength in an ever-widening circle of adventure and achievement? What man has done, the little triumphs of his present state . . . form but the prelude to the things that man has yet to do.[8]

But the outbreak of World War II shattered his illusions. He became increasingly pessimistic about man's future on the earth:

> In spite of all my disposition to a brave-looking optimism, I perceive that now the universe is bored with him, is turning

6 *Hymn of Man.*

7 *Hymn.*

8 *A Short History of the World* (Pelican Books, Harmondsworth, Middx., 1937), p. 289.

> a hard face to him, and I see him being carried less and less intelligently and more and more rapidly . . . along the stream of fate to degradation, suffering and death.

But even more shocking was the revelation of human depravity:

> But quite apart from any bodily depression, the spectacle of evil in the world — the wanton destruction of homes, the ruthless hounding of decent folk into exile, the bombings of open cities, the cold-blooded massacres and mutilations of children and defenseless gentle folk, the rapes and filthy humiliations and, above all, the return of deliberate and organized torture, mental torment and fear to a world from which such things had seemed well nigh banished — has come near to breaking my spirit altogether.[9]

By 1945 he had lost heart and lost hope. "Homo Sapiens, as he has been pleased to call himself, is played out."[10]

In the nineteenth century Tennyson wrote:

> *Move upward, working out the beast,*
> *And let the ape and tiger die.*[11]

aggressively alive.

Many were shocked to discover, in this twentieth century, that the ape and tiger had not died, and that the beast was still

The Victorians were proud of their technical achievements and were confident of the future. They were also proud of their moral achievements. Mr. Podsnap expressed the general opinion on foreign nations in the immortal words: "They do — I am sorry to be obliged to say — as they do."[12] Today we know that behind the public image of austere righteousness was a façade hiding the vast reality of prostitution. It is not surprising that their descendants, grown cynical, are tempted to reject an honor rooted in dishonor.

The Angry Young Men have taken a characteristic revenge. They enjoy attacking, with irreverent audacity, the sanctities

[9] *The Fate of Homo Sapiens* (Secker & Warburg, London, 1939), pp. 312, 107.

[10] *Mind at the End of its Tether.*

[11] *In Memoriam,* cxvii.

[12] Quoted, Bertrand Russell, in the symposium, *Ideas and Beliefs of the Victorians* (Sylvan Press, London, 1949), p. 19.

of the past. John Osborne, a highly articulate member of this group, asks: What kind of symbols do we live by? Are they truthful and worthwhile? He examines them and concludes that they are not. That is why he does not hesitate to attack the traditional paraphernalia of inherited protocol associated with the institution of the monarchy as empty and meaningless and devoid of moral and spiritual significance. "My objection to the Royal Symbol is that it is dead; it is the gold filling in a mouthful of decay." "If a man is taken in by gorgeous ceremonial and meaningless ritual he is not," he argues, "conditioned to seriousness but to totem worship."[13] John Osborne bluntly asserts that the sickly sentiment on which we have been fed is "as nourishing and useful as wax fruit under a glass case."

There is, of course, a danger in this fierce iconoclasm. To "debunk" emotion, says C. S. Lewis, is within almost anyone's capacity. The right defense against false sentiments, however, is to inculcate just sentiments. We are, he warns, in danger of producing "what may be called Men without Chests." In a characteristic passage he adds:

> You can hardly open a periodical without coming across the statement that what our civilization needs is more 'drive', or dynamism, or self-sacrifice, or 'creativity'. In a sort of ghastly simplicity we remove the organ and demand the function. We make men without chests and expect of them virtue and enterprise. We laugh at honour and are shocked to find traitors in our midst. We castrate and bid the geldings be fruitful.[14]

Lytton Strachey was the pioneer of the "science" of debunking. He set himself to destroy the reputations of the most respected members of Victorian society by a clever use of wit and ridicule. Cardinal Manning, Dr. Arnold, Florence Nightingale, General Gordon, Queen Victoria, each in turn is mockingly and maliciously derided, devalued, and exposed. Strachey achieves his purpose by subordinating historical integrity to the goal of propaganda. Using irony, cynicism,

[13] *The Encounter,* Vol. 49, October, 1957, p. 27.
[14] *The Abolition of Man* (Oxford University Press, London, 1944), p. 14.

satire, and ridicule, he creates portraits which are not only unsympathetic but unlovely.

A. E. Dyson, in a percipient article on what he calls "The Technique of Debunking," gives two examples of how Strachey does the job. He quotes Strachey's comment on the poet Clough: "This earnest adolescent, with the weak ankles and the solemn face, lived entirely with the highest ends in view." What Strachey says is that Clough was an earnest young man with the highest aims in life. What he does, however, by introducing the weak ankles, and throwing in that damaging and damning word "adolescent," is to turn him into an object of pure ridicule. Or again, there is Strachey's description of the formidable Dr. Arnold of Rugby. Strachey ridicules his subject by lumping together irrelevant trivialities with matters of real importance, the absurdity of the one being used as a weapon with which to discredit the other. At the age of thirty-three Strachey says that Dr. Arnold's "outward appearance was the index of his inward character: everything about him denoted energy, earnestness, and the best intentions. His legs, perhaps, were shorter than they should have been." The legs, in this context, make the whole man seem stunted.[15]

Lytton Strachey, by exposing with careful malice the defects of idols and the fallibility of ideals succeeded in reducing the Victorian world to a place of fallen idols and vanished ideals.

We are the residual legatees of this moral scepticism. It is now taken for granted that the Victorians were pompus hypocrites and sanctimonious humbugs. The question that we do not ask is whether we are in any better case.

William Golding insists on asking this question. Mr. Golding has a high and responsible conception of the role of the artist. "The job of the artist," he says, "is to scrape the labels off things, to take nothing for granted, to show the irrational where it exists."[16]

In *Lord of the Flies* he seeks to reveal the truth about human nature. He uses schoolboys, in the fresh innocence of youth, as a device by which to X-ray human nature. He emphatically

[15] *The Twentieth Century,* March, 1955, p. 244.
[16] I am indebted to Harry Beverly of Columbia Seminary for the interpretation which follows. See Columbia Theological Seminary *Bulletin,* Vol. LVII, no. 5, December, 1964, p. 15f.

rejects Rousseau's doctrine that the corruption of man and the sickness of society is to be attributed to the evils of civilization. On the contrary: "the basic problem of modern humanity is that of learning to live fearlessly with the natural chaos of existence." For too long, he insists, we "have never looked further than the rash appearing on the skin"; it is time we began to look "for the root of the disease instead of describing the symptoms."

Golding's purpose (in his own words) is "to trace the defects of society back to the defects of human nature." He uses as a foil R. M. Ballantyne's popular classic, *Coral Island,* which was published in 1858. In Ballantyne's novel the three boys who are shipwrecked on a tropical island live a life which is beautiful and without malice or wickedness. Golding begins with a similar setting (as befits a novel written in the mid-twentieth century, the boys are the only survivors of a plane which is destroyed in an atomic war), but the events which follow are very different. In Golding's story, the choir boys "who had said, 'Sir, yes Sir,' and who had worn caps and crosses," revert to the role of painted savages who chant a ferocious litany of hate and blood: "Kill the beast, cut his throat, spill his blood."

Golding traces the stages by which the boys succumb to tyranny and relapse into barbarism. Ralph, who is elected leader, represents the forces of law and order; Jack, who challenges his leadership, is a hunter. One by one the remnants and relics of twentieth-century civilization fall away and are discarded. Ralph knows that they can survive only if they agree on common procedures and keep the beacon alight. Jack, absorbed in the hunting of pigs, lets the fire go out, and a ship passes by. Bitter recriminations follow. The island paradise degenerates into an inferno of fear and terror. Piggy, sensing doom, tries to restore order and avert calamity. He sees, more clearly than the others, that there are only two alternatives.

> 'Which is better — to be a pack of painted niggers like you are, or to be sensible like Ralph is?'
> A great clamour rose among the savages. Piggy shouted again.

> 'Which is better — to have rules and agree, or to hunt
> and kill?'
> Again the clamour and again — 'Zup!'
> Ralph shouted against the noise.
> 'Which is better, law and rescue, or hunting and breaking
> things up?'[17]

The boys mass around him, their spears bristling. Above,
Roger levers a huge rock. It begins to move. It hurtles through
the air: the tribe shrieks: Piggy is hit a glancing blow from
head to knee; his brains spatter the rocks.

A murderous attack is immediately launched against Ralph,
who is saved from being lynched only by the arrival of the
Navy, attracted not by signal fires for rescue, but by a
barbaric blaze prepared for destructive purposes.

The naval officer who leads the landing party cannot believe
the evidence of his eyes. He is still fast bound in the world
of illusion.

> 'I should have thought,' said the officer as he visualized
> the search before him, 'I should have thought that a pack
> of British boys — you're all British aren't you? — would
> have been able to put up a better show than that — I
> mean —'
> 'It was like that at first,' said Ralph, 'before things —'
> He stopped.
> 'We were together then —'
> The officer nodded helpfully.
> 'I know. Jolly good show. Like the Coral Island.'
> Ralph looked at him dumbly. For a moment he had a
> fleeting picture of the strange glamour that had once in-
> vested the beaches. But the island was scorched up like dead
> wood — Simon was dead — and Jack had. . . . The tears
> began to flow and sobs shook him. He gave himself up
> to them now for the first time on the island; great, shudder-
> ing spasms of grief that seemed to wrench his whole body.
> His voice rose under the black smoke before the burning
> wreckage of the island; and infected by that emotion, the
> other little boys began to shake and sob too.[18]

[17] *Lord of the Flies* (Penguin Books, Harmondsworth, Middx., 1960),
p. 171.
[18] *Ibid.*, p. 192.

It is too painful. The officer, embarrassed, turns away and allows "his eyes to rest on the trim cruiser in the distance." It is typical of Golding's deep irony that the neat symbol of human rationality and inventive achievement is also the frightening symbol of man's will to destroy.

"Good symbols," it has been said, "should crystallize the intangible and clarify the obscure." Golding uses a variety of symbols to add depth and meaning to his reconstruction of the traditional story. The island itself is "boat-shaped": it represents mankind on its journey through life. One commentator explains: "The boys, representing human nature, are placed on this island, in order for Golding to hack his way through the façade of civilization to get to the tangled human dilemma where man is as he really is. Their struggle is the ancient battle between the forces of good and evil raging in every man."[19] Ralph's desperate struggle to preserve the remnants of law and order in the midst of engulfing anarchy illustrates the unhappy truth that, in this world, "powerful hands are seldom pure and pure hands seldom strong" (E. H. Robertson).

Then, in the story, there is the puzzling symbol of the beast. Initially, the beast is a symbol for the boys' primitive fears. Piggy, the intellectual, tries to persuade them that their fears are groundless: " 'Course, there isn't a beast in the forest. How could there be? What would a beast eat?" He tries again: "I know there isn't no beast — not with claws and all that, I mean — but I know there isn't no fear, either." "Unless," he adds, "we get frightened of people." Simon, who has gifts of intuitive insight which the others do not possess, understands the truth· "Maybe there is a beast. What I mean is — maybe it's only us." He becomes "inarticulate in his effort to express mankind's essential illness." When he thinks of the beast, he sees, with the clarity of inner sight, "the picture of a human at once heroic and sick." It is not surprising that Simon is the first to die in the blind orgy of a ritual murder.

Through tears and agonies and most instant perils, Ralph learns the nature of "mankind's essential sickness." He begins with a simple Pelagian faith in the goodness of natural man.

---

[19] Comment by Harry Beverly.

He has no doubt that they can live happily together, even
without adult supervision.

> 'While we're waiting we can have a good time on this
> island.'
> He gesticulated widely.
> 'It's like in a book.'
> At once there was a clamour.
> 'Treasure Island —'
> 'Swallows and Amazons —'
> 'Coral Island —'
> 'This is our island. It's a good island. Until the grown-ups
> come to fetch us we'll have fun.'[20]

As the situation steadily deteriorates, Piggy is driven to ask
the question: "What are we? Humans? Or animals? Or
savages?"

Natural man is exceedingly reluctant to admit that the world
in which we live is "East of Eden" where there is "an end of
innocence." It is Golding's supreme literary achievement that
he succeeds in persuading us that evil is nearer than hands or
feet, that evil is endemic in the heart of man.[21]

"Man," says T. E. Hulme, "is in no sense perfect, but a
wretched creature, who can yet apprehend perfection."[22] The
theological expression of this paradox is the doctrine of original
sin. "There are," Baudelaire explains, "in every man, always,
two simultaneous allegiances, one to God, the other to Satan.
Invocation of God, or Spirituality, is a desire to climb higher;
that of Satan, or animality, is delight in descent.[23] Golding,
for his part, shows us what man is like when the beast is let
off the chain. To change the metaphor: he lifts the lid. He
shows us that beneath the surface of our accomplished rationality there is a seething cauldron of untamed desire. He enables
us to explore what Robert Penn Warren, in an expressive
phrase, calls "the tractlessness of the human heart."[24]

---

[20] *Lord of the Flies*, p. 34.

[21] Mr. Golding's fifth novel, *The Spire*, was published shortly before
this book went to press. Still concerned with the problem of good and
evil, Mr. Golding this time is intent on showing the ethical ambiguity
of even our most noble deeds. Self-love and drive for power taint even
such an outwardly commendable act as arranging for a spire to be
mounted on a cathedral. Jocelyn's motives are compounded of idealism
on the one hand, and contempt for many people on the other. He

equates his strong ambition, irrational though it is, with the will of God, driving himself half-insane and exploiting people callously. The tone of the book is sympathetic, but the vision is stark and ruthlessly penetrating.

[22] "Humanism and the Religious Attitude," *Speculations* (Harcourt, Brace, New York, 1924), p. 71.

[23] *Intimate Journals,* translated by Christopher Isherwood (Methuen, London, 1949), p. 30.

[24] *Brother to Dragons,* quoted, Randall Stewart, *American Literature and Christian Doctrine* (Louisiana State University Press, Baton Rouge, 1958), p. 41.

Sodom and the Madonna

or

the impotence of the will

The heart is deceitful above all things, and desperately corrupt; who can understand it? (Jeremiah 17:9).

"I can't endure," Dostoevsky protests, in a celebrated passage, "that a man of lofty mind and heart begins with the ideal of the Madonna and ends with the ideal of Sodom. What's still more awful is that a man with the ideal of Sodom in his soul does not renounce the ideal of the Madonna, and his heart may be on fire with that ideal, genuinely on fire, just as in the days of youth and innocence." By a clever juxtaposition of disparate images — Sodom and the Madonna — Dostoevsky illustrates the truth that the man who succumbs to the sensual seductions of sin has an unhappy memory of and a restless longing for the unsullied delights of goodness and purity.

Dostoevsky, through the mouth of Mitya in *The Brothers Karamazov,* explains that to the angels was granted the vision of God's throne but to insects — "sensual lust." Mitya seizes the hand of his brother, the saintly Alyosha, and sobs: "I am that insect, brother, and to me it is said particularly. All we Karamazovs are such insects, and, angel as you are, that insect lives in you, too, and will stir up a tempest in your blood."

Within us all, Mitya repeats, there is an insect of sensuality, steadily gnawing, seeking to devour. "God and the devil are fighting there," he adds, "and the battlefield is the heart of man." "A man," Mitya sadly concludes, "always talks of his own ache."[1]

Again and again Dostoevsky reverts to the problems of depravity and perversity in the life of man. "In every man, of course, a demon lies hidden — the demon of rage, the demon of lustful heat at the screams of the tortured victim, the demon of lawlessness let off the chain, the demon of diseases that follow on vice."[2]   There are volcanic depths of evil ever waiting to erupt. "People," he comments, "talk sometimes of bestial cruelty, but that's a great injustice and insult to the beasts; a beast can never be so cruel as a man, so artistically cruel. The tiger only tears and gnaws, that's all he can do. He would never think of nailing people by the ears, even if he were able to do it."[3]

There are those who, without further reflection, subscribe to the comforting belief that man is both rational and good. The truth, Dostoevsky scornfully replies, is that much of our morality is only surface veneer, a matter of convention and convenience; beneath the surface are surging depths of lawless desire.

Robert Louis Stevenson illustrates this theme in the frightening fable of *Dr. Jekyll and Mr. Hyde*. Dr. Jekyll discovers a drug which enables him to change at will both his appearance and his nature. From being the kind, good, and respectable Dr. Jekyll, he can become the vicious, depraved, and deformed Mr. Hyde. Dr. Jekyll describes the operation of the mysterious drug: "It severed in me," he explains, "those provinces of good and ill which divide and compound man's dual nature." When he took the drug he was not play-acting. A real metamorphosis took place: "I was in no sense a hypocrite; both sides of me were in dead earnest; I was no more myself when I laid aside restraint and plunged in shame, than when I

[1] *The Brothers Karamazov,* translated by Constance Garnett (The Modern Library, New York, n.d.), p. 130.

[2] *Ibid.,* p. 297.

[3] *Ibid.,* p. 293.

laboured, in the eye of day, at the furtherance of knowledge or the relief of sorrow or suffering."[4]

Dr. Jekyll derived peculiar pleasure from these periodic excursions into his amoral self.

> There was something strange in my sensations, something indescribably new and, from its very novelty, incredibly sweet. I felt younger, lighter, happier in body; within I was conscious of a heady recklessness, a current of disordered sensual images running like a mill-race in my fancy, a solution of the bonds of obligation, an unknown but not an innocent freedom of the soul. I knew myself, at the first breath of this new life, to be more wicked, tenfold more wicked, sold a slave to my original evil; and the thought, in that moment, braced and delighted me like wine.[5]

He found increasing delight in the pursuit of forbidden pleasures. He relates:

> When I would come back from these excursions, I was often plunged into a kind of wonder at my vicarious depravity. This familiar that I called out of my own soul, and sent forth alone to do his good pleasure, was a being inherently malign and villainous; his every act and thought centered on self; drinking pleasure with bestial avidity from any degree of torture to another; relentless like a man of stone.[6]

Nevertheless, there were times when "Henry Jekyll stood aghast before the acts of Edward Hyde."

In his right mind Dr. Jekyll was a man of charity and given to religious thoughts; in the guise of Mr. Hyde he was given to blasphemy and the practice of abominable crimes. For two months he struggled to abstain from taking the drug: "for two months," he says, "I was true to my determination; for two months I led a life of such severity as I had never before attained to, and enjoyed the compensations of an approving conscience." Then he began to be "tortured with throes and longings" until, he relates, "in an hour of moral weakness, I once again compounded and swallowed the transforming

[4] *Dr. Jekyll and Mr. Hyde* (The Folio Society, London, 1948), p. 124.

[5] *Ibid.,* p. 127.

[6] *Ibid.,* p. 131.

draught." "My devil had been long caged," he says; "he came out roaring. I was conscious, even when I took the draught, of a more unbridled, a more furious propensity to ill." Again: "The spirit of hell awoke in me and raged." As destructive Mr. Hyde, he committed a senseless and sadistic murder; later, as respectable Dr. Jekyll, he was filled with horrified remorse. This time his reaction to goodness was shortlived: "as the first edge of my penitence wore off," he relates, "the lower side of me, so long indulged, so recently chained down, began to growl for licence."

He found that the thought of evil no longer filled him with alarm. "I sat in the sun on a bench; the animal within me licking the chops of memory; the spiritual side a little drowsed, promising subsequent penitence, but not yet moved to begin." Soon he began to slither further down the steep and slippery path. "I began to be aware of a change in the temper of my thoughts," he continues, "a greater boldness, a contempt of danger, a solution of the bonds of obligation." He suddenly discovered, to his horror, that the apelike thing in him had mastered him and was threatening to destroy him. Dr. Jekyll

> thought of Hyde, for all his energy of life, as of something not only hellish but inorganic. This was the shocking thing; that the slime of the pit seemed to utter cries and voices; that the amorphous dust gesticulated and sinned; that what was dead, and had no shape, should usurp the offices of life. And this again, that that insurgent horror was knit to him closer than a wife, closer than an eye; lay caged in his flesh, where he heard it mutter and felt it struggle to be born; and at every hour of weakness, and in the confidence of slumber, prevailed against him, and deposed him out of life.[7]

Dr. Jekyll explains how he learned the terrible truth that "man is not truly one, but truly two."

> It was on the moral side, and in my own person, that I learned to recognize the thorough and primitive duality of man; I saw that of the two natures that contended in the field of my consciousness, even if I could rightly be said to be either, it was only because I was radically both; and from

[7] *Ibid.*, p. 146.

an early date, even before the course of my scientific dis-
coveries had begun to suggest the most naked possibility
of such a miracle, I had learned to dwell with pleasure, as
a beloved day-dream, on the thought of the separation of
these elements. If each, I told myself, could but be housed
in separate identities, life would be relieved of all that was
unbearable; the unjust might go his way, delivered from the
aspirations and remorse of his more upright twin; and the
just could walk steadfastly and securely on his upward path,
doing the good things in which he found his pleasure, and
no longer exposed to disgrace and penitence by the hands of
this extraneous evil. It was the curse of mankind that
these incongruous fagots were thus bound together — that
in the agonised womb of consciousness these polar twins
should be continuously struggling.[8]

When Stevenson sent a copy of his novel to an American
friend, W. H. Low, he wrote: "The gnome is interesting, I
think, and he came out of a deep mine, where he guards the
fountain of tears. . . . The gnome's name is *Jekyll and Hyde;*
I believe you will find he is likewise quite willing to answer
to the name of Low or Stevenson." To John Addington Symonds he confessed: "*Jekyll* is a dreadful thing, I own." Its
subject matter, he explained, was really that "old business of
the war in the members."[9]

On one occasion Stevenson claimed that he was a psycholo-
gist or nothing. He had ground for the claim. He knew the
problems of the divided self and the reality of that "war
in the members" of which the Apostle speaks; it was, he tells
us, his aim to "shed a strong light" on that "perennial war."
It was "the only thing" he felt "dreadful about." In the words
of Henley's well-known sonnet, there was in Stevenson

> *A deal of Ariel, just a streak of Puck,*
> *Much Anthony, of Hamlet most of all.*
> *And something of the Shorter Catechist.*[10]

No doubt it was his Puritan inheritance, his familiarity with
the theology of the Shorter Catechism, which enabled Stevenson

---

8 *Ibid.,* pp. 124-5.
9 Quoted, *ibid.,* pp. 19-20.
10 *In Hospital,* XXV. Apparition.

to analyse with such extraordinary penetration the impotence of the human will.

Pascal insists that it is necessary to do justice to man's duality and to the presence of sin in the life of man.

"It is dangerous," he says wisely, "to make man see too clearly his equality with the brutes without showing him his greatness. It is also dangerous to make him see his greatness too clearly apart from his vileness. It is still more dangerous to leave him in ignorance of both. But it is very advantageous to show him both. Man must not think that he is on a level either with the brutes or with the angels, nor must he be ignorant of both sides of his nature, but he must know both."[11] Man is neither animal nor angel; on the contrary, he is a monarch who has fallen from a former high estate. "The greatness of man is so evident," Pascal suggests, "that it is even proved by his wretchedness. For what in animals is nature in man we call wretchedness; by which we recognize that, his nature being now unlike that of animals, he has fallen from a better nature which once was his."[12]

The life of man is marked by restlessness and anxiety, by discord and division. There is, says Pascal, a conflict between reason and the passions. If only man had "reason without passions . . . . If he had only passions without reason . . . . But having both, he cannot be without strife, being unable to be at peace with the one without being at war with the other." Thus, man "is always divided against, and opposed to himself."[13]

To Pascal, man (as Charles Colton puts it) is "an embodied paradox, a bundle of contradictions:"[14]

> What a chimera then is man! What a novelty! What a monster, what a chaos, what a contradiction, what a prodigy! Judge of all things, imbecile worm of the earth; depositary of truth, a sink of uncertainty and error; the pride and refuse of the universe![15]

[11] *Pensées,* No. 418.
[12] *Ibid.,* No. 409.
[13] *Ibid.,* No. 412.
[14] *Lacon,* Vol. I, No. 408.
[15] *Pensées,* No. 434.

Even in his sin, man has an awareness, Pascal says, of a lost perfection:

> If man had never been corrupt, he would enjoy in his inno-
> cence both truth and happiness with assurance; and if man
> had always been corrupt, he would have no idea of truth or
> bliss. But, wretched as we are, and more so than if there
> were no greatness in our condition, we have an idea of happi-
> ness, and cannot reach it. We perceive an image of truth,
> and possess only a lie. Incapable of absolute ignorance and
> of certain knowledge, we have thus been manifestly in a
> degree of perfection from which we have unhappily fallen.[16]

What the Christian faith affirms, the testimony of experience ratifies and confirms:

> For myself, I confess that so soon as the Christian religion
> reveals the principle that human nature is corrupt and fallen
> from God, that opens my eyes to see everywhere the mark of
> this truth: for nature is such that she testifies everywhere,
> both within man and without him, to a lost God and a cor-
> rupt nature.[17]

In the life of every man there are, Pascal points out, tragic schisms and latent contradictions. Every man is a creature, not only of ambiguity but of perversity, not only of duality but of depravity, not only of contradiction but of corruption. "We know and approve the better," Ovid sadly confesses, "and do the worse."[18] "Man is neither angel nor brute," Pascal ob-serves, "and the unfortunate thing is that he who would act the angel acts the brute."[19]

James Boswell notes in his *Diary* for Sunday, November 28, 1762: "I went to St. James's Church and heard service and a good sermon on 'By what means shall a young man learn to order his ways,' in which the advantages of early piety were well displayed. What a curious, inconsistent thing is the mind of man! In the midst of divine service I was laying plans for having women, and yet I had the most sincere feelings of

---

[16] *Ibid.*
[17] *Ibid.*, No. 441.
[18] *Metamorphoses* vii, 20.
[19] *Pensées,* No. 358.

religion."[20] Boswell was not destitute of religious instincts; he had a desire Godward; but he was not able to banish from his mind the seductive delights of sin.

The Apostle Paul knew what it is to be torn asunder by conflicting desires. "I delight in the law of God, in my inmost self," he insists, but "I see in my members another law at war with the law of my mind and making me captive to the law of sin which dwells in my members." "I do not understand my own actions," he explains unhappily, "for I do not do what I want but I do the very thing I hate." "I can will what is right," he continues, "but I cannot do it. For I do not do the good I want, but the evil I do not want is what I do." When he wants "to do right," he explains, he finds that "evil lies close at hand." He lacks the strength, he sadly confesses, to do that which he knows to be right (Romans 7:15ff.). Francis Quarles puts the matter in epigrammatic form.

> I like, dislike, lament for what I could not;
> I do, undo, yet still do what I should not;
> And, at the self same instant, will the
> thing I would not.

In his unregenerate days Augustine had the same unhappy experience. "I was at strife with myself and rent asunder by myself."

> I was bound, not with another's irons, but by my own iron will. My will the enemy held, and thence had made a chain for me, and bound me. For of a forward will was a lust made; and a lust served, became custom; and custom not resisted, became necessity. By which links, as it were, joined together (wherein I called it a chain) a hard bondage held me enthralled.[21]

He was in a state of moral paralysis, impotent to do that which he knew to be right.

> When Thou didst on all sides show me that which Thou saidst was true, I, convicted by the truth, had nothing at all to answer, but only those dull and drowsy words, "Anon,

[20] *Boswell's London Journal 1762-1763* (Wm. Heinemann, London, 1950), p. 62.
[21] *Confessions* viii, 5, 10.

anon," "presently," "leave me but a little." But "presently" had no present, and my "little while" went on for a long while. . . . For the law of sin is the violence of custom, whereby the wind is drawn and holden, even against its will.[22]

Like the Apostle Paul, Augustine was constrained to cry: "Wretched man that I am! Who will deliver me from this body of death?" (Romans 7:24) The deliverance which he sought, he found in Christ. With the Apostle Paul he was able to say: "Thanks be to God, who gives us the victory through our Lord Jesus Christ" (1 Corinthians 15:57).

[22] *Ibid.,* viii, 5, 12.

An Awareness of Solitude

or

the horror of alienation

I shall be a fugitive and a wanderer on the earth
(Genesis 4:14).

Henri Bergson says that in the soul of the desperate criminal there is always a feeling of remorse, arising from a desire, "not so much to evade punishment as to wipe out the past, to arrange things just as though the crime had never been committed." That is why a criminal will often seek someone to whom he can confess:

> By thus putting himself right, if not in the eyes of all, at least in somebody's eyes, he re-attaches himself to society at a single point, by a thread: even if he does not reinstate himself in it, at least he is near it, close to it; he no longer remains alienated from it; in any case he is no longer in complete rupture with it, nor with that element of it which is part of himself.[1]

Alienation is always a consequence of sin. Ernest Hemingway illustrates this fact in his novel *For Whom the Bell Tolls*. The story is set in the context of the Spanish Civil War. Pablo,

[1] *The Two Sources of Morality and Religion* (Doubleday Anchor Books, New York, n.d.), p. 18.

who is the leader of a small Republican band operating behind
the Fascist lines, is guilty of an act of calculated treachery and
betrayal.   He is, by nature, a shifty, unreliable opportunist.
He deserts, taking with him the dynamite they need to blow
up the bridge.   His wife, Pilar, is a woman of astonishing determination.   She is as resolute as her husband is weak.   She
is under no illusions about her husband's duplicity.   Pablo,
after an interval of some days, unexpectedly returns.   Pilar
regards him with mocking contempt.   He shamefacedly blurts
out: "Having done such a thing there is a loneliness which
cannot be borne."[2]

He has come back, he tells her, because he cannot endure
the loneliness, the sense of being cut off, the experience of
alienation.

It is the tragic theme of alienation and estrangement which
provides the subject matter of much twentieth-century existen-
tialist literature.   Nathan Scott draws attention to the fact
that the image of man which recurs most frequently today is
man in his isolation and loneliness, and he quotes Melville's
description of the Islanders in the Pequod as aptly descriptive
of man in contemporary society: "*Isolatoes,* I call such, not
acknowledging the common continent of men, but each *Isolato*
living in a separate continent of his own."[3]   In this twentieth
century we are all, in our loneliness and guilt, "displaced
persons."   We are both restless and rootless.   William Faulkner,
in *Light in August,* says of Joe Christmas, the hunted mulatto,
"there was something rootless about him, as though no town
or city was his, no street, no walls, no square of earth his
home."[4]   It is an apt description of alienated man in the frac-
tured world of today.

Within the neurotic life of modern, urbanized society, we are
being increasingly made aware of the problem of human loneliness.   David Riesman gives his sociological study of contemporary society the descriptive title *The Lonely Crowd.*   According
to Rabbinic tradition Cain was the first builder of cities, and

[2] *For Whom the Bell Tolls* (Jonathan Cape, London, 1942), p. 367.
[3] Quoted, *Modern Literature and the Religious Frontier* (Harper,
New York, 1958), p. 72.
[4] Quoted, *ibid.*

it is the city itself which is today pre-eminently the symbol of despair. Shelley says prophetically,

> *Hell is a city much like London —*
> *A populous and smoky city.*[5]

Lewis Mumford, in *The Culture of Cities,* entitles one of his most penetrating chapters, "A Brief Outline of Hell." In hell no community is possible, no meaningful fellowship, no personal relationships.

Jean-Paul Sartre makes this point, with impressive power, in his one-act play *No Exit.* The setting is the seedy living room of a second-rate hotel with hideous Second Empire furniture. There are no windows and no mirrors: there is only a glaring electric light bulb which never goes out. There are three characters, and they are doomed to eternal wakefulness: Garcin, a military coward who has been shot; Inez, a lesbian; and Estelle, a nymphomaniac, who has murdered her child. They realize they are in hell. They are surprised at first to find none of the proverbial fires nor instruments of torture. They soon discover, however, that they are to be their own tormentors. They desperately seek to hide the unedifying facts about themselves from each other. It is Inez who compels them to face the horrid truth.

> INEZ: Look here! What's the point of play-acting, trying to throw dust in each other's eyes? We're all tarred with the same brush.
>
> ESTELLE (*indignantly*): How dare you!
>
> INEZ: Yes, we are criminals — murderers — all three of us. We're in hell, my pets; they never make mistakes, and people aren't damned for nothing
>
> ESTELLE: Stop! For heaven's sake —
>
> INEZ: In hell! Damned souls — that's us all three!
>
> ESTELLE: Keep quiet! I forbid you to use such disgusting words.
>
> INEZ: A damned soul — that's you, my little plaster saint. And ditto our friend there, the noble pacifist. We've had our hour of pleasure, haven't we? There have been people who burned their lives out for our sakes — and

5 *Peter Bell the Third,* pt. 3, Hell, i.

we chuckled over it. So now we have to pay the reckoning.

GARCIN (*raising his fist*): Will you keep your mouth shut, damn it!

INEZ (*confronting him fearlessly, but with a look of vast surprise*): Well, well! (*A pause.*) Ah, I understand now. I know why they've put us three together.

GARCIN: I advise you to — to think twice before you say any more.

INEZ: Wait! You'll see how simple it is. Childishly simple. Obviously there aren't any physical torments — you agree, don't you? And yet we're in hell. And no one else will come here. We'll stay in this room together, the three of us, for ever and ever . . . In short, there's someone absent here, the official torturer.

GARCIN (*sotto voice*): I'd noticed that.

INEZ: It's obvious what they're after — an economy of manpower — or devil-power, if you prefer. The same idea as in the cafeteria, where customers serve themselves.

ESTELLE: What ever do you mean?

INEZ: I mean that each of us will act as torturer of the two others.[6]

They realize that their condition is infernal. There is no escape from this hell of being eternally together and yet eternally alienated. The male member of the trio sums up the unpleasant reality of the situation: "Hell is — other people."

In hell there are no personal relationships, there is no community. What is hell? Dostoevsky asks, and he makes the profound reply: "It is the suffering of being unable to love."[7] In hell, each is isolated from the other, each is an island, an island of egocentricity, an island of tormenting loneliness and guilt. George Macdonald says: "The one principle of hell is — 'I am my own.'"[8] Edward Chamberlayne, in *The Cocktail Party,* says:

[6] *No Exit and Three Other Plays* (Vintage Books, New York, 1955), p. 17.

[7] *The Brothers Karamazov,* translated by Constance Garnett (Modern Library, New York, n.d.), p. 400.

[8] Quoted, *George Macdonald: An Anthology,* edited, C. S. Lewis (Geoffrey Bles, London, 1946), p. 85.

> *Hell is oneself*
> *Hell is alone, the other figures in it*
> *Merely projections. There is nothing to escape from*
> *And nothing to escape to. One is always alone.*[9]

It is the problem of loneliness which Sartre further explores in his philosophical novel *Nausea*. It is written in the form of the diary of one Antoine Roquentin, who is working on the biography of the Marquis de Rollebon. Antoine has no commitments, no family responsibilities, no financial anxieties. And yet he is unutterably depressed: he has intermittent spasms of nausea, vertigo, acute anxiety, and other forms of nervous tension which, in the Sartrian universe, says Maurice Cranston, "are not so much symptoms of psychological disorder as intimations of metaphysical reality."[10]

Antoine contemplates his face in a mirror, and confides to his diary:

> I can understand nothing of this face. The faces of others have some sense, some direction. Not mine. I cannot even decide whether it is handsome or ugly. I think it is ugly because I have been told so. But it doesn't strike me.

Later, in the same entry, Roquentin writes:

> Perhaps it is impossible to understand one's own face. Or perhaps it is because I am a single man? People who live in society have learned how to see themselves in mirrors as they appear to their friends. I have no friends. Is that why my flesh is so naked?[11]

His feelings (which he cannot explicate) culminate in an overwhelming and all-pervading sense of nausea. He begins to realize that the problems from which he suffers are not so much external to himself as within himself: "It holds me . . . the nausea is not inside me. . . . I am the one who is within it."[12] Finally, he comes to the conclusion that freedom is not

9 T. S. Eliot, *The Complete Poems and Plays 1909-1950* (Harcourt, Brace, New York, 1952), p. 342.

10 *Sartre* (Oliver & Boyd, Edinburgh, 1962), p. 14.

11 *Nausea*, translated by Lloyd Alexander (New Directions Books, Norfolk, Conn., 1959), pp. 27, 29.

12 *Ibid.*, p. 170.

to be found in running away from engagement and commit-
ment. He goes to Paris to see his former mistress, Anny, who
has invited him to visit her. She is now living with an Egyp-
tian. They talk together of their past life together. She protests that she has outlived herself. Roquentin wonders what
to say to her. He finally tells himself: "I can do nothing for
her; she is as solitary as I."[13]

Sartre is preoccupied with the problem of human freedom.
How can a man achieve authentic existence? How can a man
break out of the iron circle of his own egocentricity? The
problem, as Sartre appreciates, is not simply moral but also
metaphysical. Christianity says the same. It insists that the
tragedy of human existence is not only that man is a stranger
on earth but also that he is an exile from heaven. "Your iniq-
uities," says the prophet Isaiah, "have made a separation between you and your God, and your sins have hid his face
from you so that he does not hear" (Isaiah 59:2). Man,
in his alienation, is cut off from God. It is this which adds the
dimension of terror.

Can a man scale the ramparts of heaven and win acceptance?
Is there a bridgehead into the presence of God? Is it possible,
in the language of the New Testament, to break down "the
dividing wall of hostility" (Ephesians 2:14)? Is there a way
back? Can the past be undone?

T. S. Eliot explores the deeper implications of alienation
in his sophisticated verse play *The Cocktail Party*. Celia Coplestone visits the psychiatrist, Harcourt-Reilly, and tells him that
she has two symptoms. She explains that, in the first place,
she has "an awareness of solitude." She admits that this expression of the situation sounds flat. She attempts to be more
explicit.

> *I mean that what has happened has made me aware*
> *That I've always been alone. That one is always alone.*
> *Not simply the ending of one relationship,*
> *Not even simply finding that it never existed —*
> *But a revelation about my relationship*
> *With everybody. Do you know —*
> *It no longer seems worthwhile to speak to anyone!*

[13] *Ibid.,* p. 203.

Reilly asks whether she really doesn't want to see anybody any more, and she replies:

> No ... it isn't that I want to be alone,
> But that everyone's alone — or so it seems to me.
> They make noises, and think they are talking to each other;
> They make faces, and think they understand each other.
> And I'm sure that they don't.

Reilly asks about her other symptom. Celia replies:

> That's stranger still.
> It sounds ridiculous — but the only word for it
> That I can find, is a sense of sin.
> REILLY: You suffer from a sense of sin, Miss Coplestone?
> This is most unusual.
> CELIA: It seemed to me abnormal.
> REILLY: Tell me what you mean by a sense of sin.
> CELIA: Its much easier to tell you what I don't mean: I
> don't mean sin in the ordinary sense.

She is asked to be more precise. She continues:

> Well, my bringing up was pretty conventional —
> I had always been taught to disbelieve in sin.
> Oh, I don't mean that it was ever mentioned!
> But anything wrong, from our point of view,
> Was either bad form, or was psychological.
> And bad form always led to disaster
> Because the people one knew disapproved of it.
> I don't worry much about form, myself —
> But when everything's bad form, or mental kinks,
> You either become bad form, and cease to care,
> Or else, if you care, you must be kinky.[14]

She is deeply convinced that her feeling of guilt is not a "kink." She speculates for a moment whether perhaps it is some kind of hallucination, but she immediately dismisses the idea: "I'm frightened by the fear that it is more real than anything I believed in." She can neither evade it nor ignore it. She says that she has a feeling "of emptiness, of failure towards some-

---

[14] Eliot, op. cit., pp. 360-1.

one, or something, outside of myself"; and then she says: "I feel I must . . . *atone* — is that the word?"

Celia Coplestone is aware of her lonely alienation and guilt. She knows that she needs, and needs desperately, absolution and atonement.

Kafka explores these themes in his frightening and disturbing novels, *The Trial* and *The Castle*. According to W. H. Auden, Kafka is the representative writer of the twentieth century, in the same way that Dante is the representative writer of the fourteenth century, and Shakespeare of the sixteenth century, and Goethe of the nineteenth century. Kafka, he insists, is *the* representative writer of the twentieth century.[15]

Kafka's writing is essentially autobiographical. He projects and universalizes his own poignant personal experiences. His attitude to his father was, we learn, ambivalent. Towards his father he felt the contrary and contradictory emotions of both love and loathing, gratitude and resentment. Writing to his father, he confesses: "My writings were about you, in them I merely poured out the lamentations I could not pour out on your breast." In the presence of his father he felt, he says, "an infinite sense of guilt."[16]

In Kafka's relationship to his father we have a symbolic picture, a paradigm, of guilty man's fear in relation to God. In the presence of God we all tend to feel, as Kafka felt in relation to his father, an infinite sense of guilt. At one moment we desire to find God, at the next to flee from Him. We protest vehemently that we want to be left alone, and yet the very thing we most fear is the dread possibility of being left alone. Our deep ambivalence is reflected in Cain's explosive anger in relation to God. "In Cain," writes Oliver Quick, "there appears for the first time that perennial conflict in the soul of fallen man, the conflict between the passionate claim to be left alone, the assertion of independence, and the no less passionate terror of being left alone, the obscure foreboding of the hell to which independence leads. The first produces the

---

[15] Quoted, W. B. J. Martin, "Significant Modern Writers: Franz Kafka," *The Expository Times* (T. & T. Clark, Edinburgh), July 1960, p. 309.

[16] Quoted, Max Brod, *Franz Kafka* (Schocken, New York, 1960), p. 24.

indignant question, Am I my brother's keeper? the second, the bitter complaint, Behold, thou hast driven me out this day from the face of the earth, and from thy face I shall be hid.[17]

Like Cain, we are conscious at one and the same time of defiance and desire. According to Helmut Thielicke "the wish to be free of God is the deepest yearning of man. It is greater than his yearning for God."[18] Francis Thompson, in his strangely haunting poem, tells the story of how he sought to flee from God, and of how he found himself relentlessly pursued by the "Hound of Heaven."

> I fled Him, down the nights and down the days;
>   I fled Him, down the arches of the years;
> I fled Him, down the labyrinthine ways
>   Of my own mind; and in the mist of tears
> I hid from Him, and under running laughter.
>   Up vistaed hopes I sped;
>   And shot, precipitated,
> Adown Titanic glooms of chasmed fear,
>   From those strong Feet that followed, followed after.
>
> But with unhurrying chase,
>   And unperturbèd pace,
> Deliberate speed, majestic instancy,
>   They beat — and a Voice beat,
>   More instant than the Feet —
> "All things betray thee, who betrayeth Me."

C. S. Lewis has described his reluctant confrontation with Christ. That night, in Magdalen College, Oxford, he was conscious, he says, "of the steady, unrelenting approach of Him whom I so earnestly desired not to meet." "That which I greatly feared had at last come upon me . . . . I gave in, and admitted that God was God and knelt and prayed: perhaps, that night, the most dejected and reluctant convert in all England. . . . The hardness of God is kinder than the softness of men, and His compulsion is our liberation."[19]

Edwin Muir, through whose enterprise and industry the works of Kafka have been made available to English readers,

17 *The Gospel of the New World* (Nisbet, London, 1944), p. 40.
18 *Nihilism* (Harper & Row, New York, 1961).
19 *Surprised by Joy* (Geoffrey Bles, London, 1955), p. 215.

describes the experiences of the anonymous person who is the subject matter of Kafka's tormented novels.

> He looks ahead and sees, perhaps on a distant hill, a shape which he has often seen before in his journey, but always far away, and apparently inaccessible; that shape is justice, grace, truth, final reconciliation, father, God. As he gazes at it he wonders whether he is moving towards it while it is receding from him, or flying from it while it is pursuing him. He is tormented by this question, for it is insoluble by human reasoning. He feels irresistibly drawn towards that distant shape, and yet cannot overcome his dread of it.

According to Edwin Muir, Kafka, in *The Castle,* describes the struggle to reach it, and in *The Trial,* the flight from it. But the hero can neither reach it nor escape it.[20]

The Trial opens with the words: "Someone must have been telling lies about Joseph K., for without having done anything wrong he was arrested one fine morning." The hero is chief clerk in a bank, and is referred to throughout the book by his initial, as though he was deficient in personality, in family background and status — as indeed he proves to be, for he is the typical uprooted displaced person. The "arrest" takes place on the morning of his thirtieth birthday. Albert Camus says that the age of thirty is a crucial period in a man's life, when it becomes impossible for a man to ignore the threat of time or to fool himself about his achievements.[21] It is clear that Kafka intends this startling event to stand for the middle point in human life, an abrupt jolt into crisis. But at no point in the story is K. told the nature of his crime, nor does he ever come face to face with the judge, nor does his arrest ever take him right out of the familiar workaday world, to which, however, he now sustains a new and bizarre relationship.

At first K. tries to deal with the situation along familiar lines: he supposes it must be a practical joke played upon him

[20] *Essays on Literature and Society* (Hogarth Press, London, 1949), p. 121.

[21] *The Myth of Sisyphus and Other Essays* (Vintage Books, New York, 1959). Quoted W. R. Mueller, *The Prophetic Voice in Modern Fiction,* p. 103.

by his office friends. Then he tries another tack: it is all a mistake, a blunder committed at headquarters (wherever that is!). He asks the two men sent to apprehend him for their credentials, but they only laugh; he tries to produce his own, but they have mysteriously disappeared. Pulling himself together, he thinks, "It will be all right if I can see someone in authority, not these ignorant menials." But the situation gets worse instead of better. The more rational he strives to be, the more irrational the situation becomes. As the case proceeds, he begins to brood over his past, to analyse his relationships with other people, to analyse himself lest some secret flaw, some unconscious betrayal, has landed him in this plight. "To ask questions is surely the main thing," he says, but what questions? That in itself now becomes a problem. Finally, after many disconcerting, nightmare experiences, during which clichés he has used a hundred times fall to pieces on his lips, he is carried off, stabbed to the heart by his warder, "like a dog." Nevertheless, just before the fatal stab he sees a human figure leaning out of a high and distant window toward him and stretching out both arms. K. responds by raising his hands and spreading out all his fingers.

W. B. J. Martin quotes John Middleton Murry's memorable saying: "A truly great novel is a tale to the simple, a parable to the wise, and a direct revelation of reality to the man who has made it a part of his being," and adds these suggestive comments:

> On one level, *The Trial* is a tale, almost a satire on the growingly familiar world of bureaucracy, with its tortuous ramifications and frustrations, a sort of Czechoslovakian *Little Dorrit,* complete with its Circumlocution Office and its maddening delays and buck-passing. Kafka's experience in the Workers' Accident Insurance Office in Prague undoubtedly provided him with rich material here. This world is one in which paper has ousted people, and statistics are more important than souls, a world where the Little Man's life is ruled by powers known only by name, never in face-to-face contact.
>
> But the tale is certainly not for the simple. It only begins to cohere when it is regarded as a parable of the human situation. It declares that man lives on two levels, in two worlds, which have the strange power of mocking and mysti-

fying one another. So Joseph K. suddenly finds the safe,
substantial framework of his daily life, the world of the
bank in which he was at home, capable and confident, becoming unreal and hostile. When he is transported to the
other world, the world of the Court, his mind, which was
such a reliable instrument in dealing with finance, accounts,
industrial problems, only flounders when it has to deal with
the problems presented by the Law Court; not only does he
fail to find the answers, he is unable even to understand the
questions or to frame questions that will make sense. "Somebody has been telling lies about Joseph K." But were they
lies after all? Gradually, Joseph ceases to ponder the question of guilt and innocence; now the question becomes,
"Guilty or innocent, how do I satisfy the Law?" On this
level the book might be read as a commentary on the doctrine of Justification by Faith. It deals with precisely the
same problem that haunted the Apostle Paul, but it only
poses the problem in a specially modern manner, it does not
come up with a solution.[22]

Kafka wrote in his *Diaries,* "Sometimes I feel I understand
the Fall of Man better than anyone," and, again, "The state in
which we find ourselves is sinful, quite independent of guilt."[23]
It is with this problem that his books deal; and it is this problem which Kafka remorselessly seeks to explore. As W. B. J.
Martin further comments:

> *The Trial* can be read on the third level as "a direct revela-
> tion of reality to the man who has made it a part of his
> being." The writings of Kafka everywhere show evidence
> that they were "a part of his being". He himself took to
> writing as a way of salvation. "My writing", he wrote, "is
> a form of prayer"; it was his attempt to externalize the night-
> mare of alienation and to win some measure of control
> over it.
>
> The section of the novel in which Kafka comes closest
> to a religious solution is that entitled "In the Cathedral". . . .
> Joseph K. finds himself in the cathedral, having been sent
> there by the Bank to meet a client who never appears. As
> he is on the point of leaving, a strong voice calls his name

22 "Significant Modern Writers: Franz Kafka," *The Expository Times*
(T. & T. Clark, Edinburgh), July 1960, pp. 309-11.
23 Franz Kafka, *The Great Wall of China* (Schocken, New York,
1960), p. 298.

from the pulpit of the darkened building, and a young priest proceeds to offer him advice on his plight. Among other things he says that K. is depending too much on outside help, the wrong kind of help, whereupon K. turns away in a huff, but is recalled by an agonized shriek. The priest cries out, "Can't you see one step before you!", as if addressing a man walking to his doom. So K., startled and impressed, begs the priest to come down from the pulpit to give him personal advice. . . .

When they are both seated, the priest embarks on a long and very detailed parable, one of the greatest parables in modern literature. . . . The parable concerns a man from the country who seeks admission to the Law. Before the Law stands a doorkeeper on guard, who keeps him there for days, months, years, until finally the man, aged and frail, dies on the radiant threshold. Before he dies, he asks the door-keeper how it is that through all the years of waiting he has seen no other applicant for admission, whereupon the doorman replies: "No one but you could gain admittance through this door, since the door was intended only for you. I am now going to shut it."

K.'s immediate reaction is to analyse the parable, but every attempt he makes is dismissed by the priest, who tells him that he is like so many commentators on Scripture, who advance theories but refuse to confront the facts. He compares K. to the man in the parable who spent his life examining theories and was too exhausted and wasted to make direct contact with reality.[24]

The meaning of the parable, comments William Mueller, is that salvation is absolutely beyond the power of man. It is futile to argue an innocence which does not exist and to look to oneself or any other human being for an acquittal which it is not his to give. Nevertheless, however inaccessible it may seem, there *is* a "radiance that streams inextinguishably from the door of the Law." Man cannot save himself but there is a radiance which has the power of salvation.[25]

The problems which Kafka attributes to his pseudonymous character K. were also the problems of his own life. "I was

[24] W. B. J. Martin, *op. cit.,* pp. 309-11.
[25] *The Prophetic Voice in Modern Fiction* (Association Press, New York, 1959), p. 109.

an outcast," he confesses to his father, "condemned, defeated,
and although I struggled my utmost to flee elsewhere, it was
labor in vain, because I was trying to do something that was
impossible, that was beyond my strength."[26]

Kafka, according to Max Brod, disputes with God as Job
once did. How can a man find God? In his desperate anguish, Job is moved to protest:

> For he is not a man, as I am, that I might answer him,
>   that we should come to trial together.
> There is no umpire between us,
>   who might lay his hand upon us both (Job 9:32-33).

This is Kafka's problem: how can he win an acquittal? Who
will intercede for him? Is there a savior? At the end of
The Trial K. becomes aware that there *is* a faraway, unknown,
indistinct person:

> His glance fell on the top story of the house adjoining the
> quarry. With a flicker as of a light going up, the casements
> of a window there suddenly flew open; a human figure, faint
> and insubstantial at that distance and that height, leaned ab-
> ruptly forward and stretched both arms still farther. Who
> was it? A friend? A good man? Someone who sympa-
> thised? Someone who wanted to help? Was it one person
> only? Or were they all there? Was help at hand?[27]

Kafka insists that a man cannot live without "permanent
faith." But how is a man to get faith — faith which is "like
a guillotine, as heavy and as light"? Kafka says that there
is a chariot by which a man can be saved. In one of his
meditations, Kafka writes: "Hold fast! . . . then you too will
see the unchangeable, dark distance, out of which nothing
can come except one day the chariot; it rolls out, gets bigger
and bigger, fills the whole world at the moment it reaches you
— and you sink into it like a child sinking into the upholstery
of a carriage that drives through storm and night."[28] These
words are strangely reminiscent of the haunting words of the
Negro spiritual with its suggestion of divine rescue and re-

[26] Max Brod, *op. cit.*, p. 25.
[27] *The Trial* (Penguin Books, Harmondsworth, Middx., 1953), p. 250.
[28] Max Brod, *op. cit.*, pp. 172-3.

demption: "Swing low, sweet chariot, coming for to carry me home."

The Trial is an exploration of the problem of guilt. K. comes to a sudden conviction of sin. His feeling of unrest is caused by a sudden awareness of uncleanness, not growing out of any specific identifiable crime, but out of his first shattering apprehension of the human condition. He marks his discovery by breakfasting on "a fine apple." The Biblical overtones cannot be ignored. K., conscious of his guilt, desires to plead his case before the court in the tenement attic of the city. He errs, however, in thinking that any human court can grant him an acquittal. "The Court wants nothing from you," the priest says. "It receives you when you come and it dismisses you when you go."

Again, it is the problem of loneliness which Kafka explores in *The Castle*. The hero, who is simply called K., in autobiographical fashion, passes through life alone. A surveyor by profession, he seeks to settle in a village, but to do this, he needs the permission of the castle. He finds the castle barred against him, and he also finds that the peasants are hostile to him and turn their backs: "Nobody can be the companion of anyone here," he is told. The castle, in the symbolism of the novel, stands for divine guidance, and the peasants for mother earth. He discovers that he is not only an exile from heaven but a stranger on the earth. "I have been here quite a long time and am already feeling a little deserted," he complains to the schoolmaster. "To the peasants I don't belong and to the castle I don't either, I suppose." "Between the peasants and the castle there is no difference," the schoolmaster replies.

St. Paul reminds the Ephesians that there was a time when they were "separated from Christ, alienated from the commonwealth of Israel, and strangers to the covenants of promise, having no hope and without God in the world" (Ephesians 2:12). Writing to the Colossians the Apostle repeats the charge: "You [were] once estranged and hostile in mind, doing evil deeds" (Colossians 1:21). Every unregenerate man is in a state of alienation which speaks, with grim foreboding, of a more dreadful alienation yet to come. In hell, Jesus says, in words of awful solemnity, their worm does not die and the fire is not quenched. "The great cries of the

soul in literature and in life," says John A. Hutton, "are the
cries of those who are afraid of that loneliness" — that loneliness which is a consequence of the averted face of God —
"or who are already tasting the bitterness of it."[29]

29 *Ancestral Voices* (Hodder & Stoughton, London, 1915), p. 238.

Who Killed Cock Robin?

or

the indelibility of guilt

What have you done? (Genesis 4:10).

"A few actions," says F. W. Robertson of Brighton, in a celebrated sermon, "often decide the destiny of individuals because they settle the tone and form of mind from which there will be in this life no alteration. . . . In those mysterious chapters at the commencement of the book of Genesis," he continues, "we are told that it was one act which sealed the destiny of Adam and of all the human race."[1]

It is often through one decisive event that a man's character is revealed, whether in irreparable weakness or heroic strength. For the Chaplain, in Bernard Shaw's *St. Joan,* the moment of blinding self-revelation was the actual burning of the Maid. In the light of the flames he saw, for the first time, the depths of his own sinful fanaticism. During the course of the trial he had repeatedly insisted that the Maid must be burned. He was bitterly indignant when she was permitted to sign a reluctant retraction. "My Lord," he protested, "do you mean that you are going to allow this woman to escape us?"

---

[1] *Sermons Preached at Trinity Chapel, Brighton* (Smith, Elder & Co., London, 1866), Vol. IV, p. 333.

When Joan tore her retraction in pieces, he cried exultantly: "Light your fire, man. To the stake with her." When she was ordered to be taken from the court to the field, he was one of the first to rush forward, shouting: "Into the fire with the witch!"

In the lurid light of the flames he saw, for the first time, his own sin. He fled from the accursed scene, his conscience aflame with guilt. Stumbling into the presence of the Duke of Warwick, he cried: "My lord, my lord: for Christ's sake pray for my wretched guilty soul. . . . I meant no harm. I did not know what it would be like. . . . I did not know what I was doing. I am a hot-headed fool; and I shall be damned to all eternity." Warwick tried to calm him: "Nonsense! Very distressing, no doubt; but it was not your doing." The Chaplain knew better; he knew his own awful culpability and guilt. He bitterly cried:

> I let them do it. If I had known, I would have torn her from their hands. You don't know: you havn't seen: it is so easy to talk when you don't know. You madden yourself with words: you damn yourself because it feels grand to throw oil on the flaming hell of your own temper. But when it is brought home to you; when you see the thing you have done; when it is blinding your eyes, stifling your nostrils, tearing your heart, then — then — (*Falling on his knees*) O God, take away this sight from me! O Christ, deliver me from this fire that is consuming me! She cried to Thee in the midst of it: Jesus! Jesus! Jesus! She is in Thy bosom; and I am in hell for evermore.[2]

For Jean-Baptiste Clamence, in Camus' story *The Fall,* the moment of painful self-discovery, of uncomfortable self-illumination, took place late at night when he was crossing the Pont Royal. This is the story as he relates it:

> I was returning to the Left Bank and my home by way of the Pont Royal. It was an hour past midnight, a fine rain was falling, a drizzle rather, that scattered the few people on the streets. I had just left a mistress, who was surely already asleep. I was enjoying that walk, a little numbed, my body calmed and irrigated by a flow of blood gentle as the

[2] *St. Joan* (Penguin Books, Harmondsworth, Middx., 1946), pp. 169-70.

falling rain. On the bridge I passed behind a figure leaning over the railing and seeming to stare at the river. On closer view, I made out a slim young woman dressed in black. The back of her neck, cool and damp between her dark hair and coat collar, stirred me. But I went on after a moment's hesitation. At the end of the bridge I followed the quays toward Saint-Michel, where I lived. I had already gone some fifty yards when I heard the sound — which, despite the distance, seemed dreadfully loud in the midnight silence — of a body striking the water. I stopped short, but without turning around. Almost at once I heard a cry, repeated several times, which was going downstream; then it suddenly ceased. The silence that followed, as the night suddenly stood still, seemed interminable. I wanted to run and yet didn't stir. I was trembling, I believe from cold and shock. I told myself that I had to be quick and I felt an irresistible weakness steal over me. I have forgotten what I thought then. "Too late, too far . . ." or something of the sort. I was still listening as I stood motionless. Then, slowly under the rain, I went away. I informed no one.[3]

At the time this incident occurred, Clamence was practising as a successful lawyer in Paris. Professionally, he accepted the cases of the poor and defenseless; privately, he was known to be kind to the aged and generous to beggars. "I never accepted a bribe," he tells us, "and I never stooped either to any shady proceedings. . . ." "I never charged the poor a fee and never boasted of it." He continues:

> I loved to help blind people cross streets. From as far away as I could see a cane hesitating on the edge of a sidewalk, I would rush forward, sometimes only a second ahead of another charitable hand already oustretched, snatch the blind person from any solicitude but mine, and lead him gently but firmly along the crosswalk among the traffic obstacles toward the refuge of the other sidewalk, when we would separate with equal emotion. My courtesy . . . . was famous and unquestionable. . . . I was considered generous, and so I was.

On the bridge that fateful night, Clamence came to a sudden awareness of the unflattering truth about himself. He realised,

---

[3] *The Fall* (Vintage Books, New York, 1956), pp. 69-70.

for the first time, that he had been wearing "a double face," that he was, in fact, only "a charming Janus." He realised that he had actually never performed a good deed without an ulterior motive. "When I would leave a blind man on the sidewalk to which I had convoyed him," he relates, "I used to tip my hat to him. Obviously the hat tipping wasn't intended for him, since he couldn't see it. To whom was it addressed? To the public. After playing my part, I would take the bow." He says, further, "I occasionally pretended to take life seriously. But very soon the frivolity of seriousness struck me and I merely went on playing my role as well as I could. I played at being efficient, intelligent, virtuous, civic-minded, shocked, indulgent, fellowspirited, edifying. . . ." Sports and acting were the only things about which he was really sincere and enthusiastic. "Even now," he confesses, "the Sunday matches in an overflowing stadium, and the theatre, which I love with the greatest passion, are the only places in the world where I feel innocent."

The event on the bridge marked, for Clamence, the beginning of salutary self-knowledge. Like Adam and Eve after their disobedience, the discovery of what he was made him feel guilty and afraid. "I was aware of the dissonances and disorders that filled me; I felt vulnerable and open to public discussion." Clamence became conscious of the secret and satiric laughter of his friends: in their presence he felt naked and exposed. He realized it was part of the necessary price which he had to pay for growth in self-knowledge. "They had to teach me," he explains, "to see clearly within me and to discover at last that I was not simple."

On another occasion he was on a bridge, shortly after dark. He felt an ineffable sense of exaltation when again he heard laughter.

> I had gone up on the Pont des Arts, deserted at that hour, to look at the river that could hardly be made out now night had come. Facing the statue of the Vert-Galant, I dominated the island. I felt rising within me a vast feeling of power and — I don't know how to express it — of com-pletion, which cheered my heart. I straightened up and was about to light a cigarette, the cigarette of satisfaction, when, at that very moment, a laugh burst out behind me. Taken

by surprise, I suddenly wheeled around: there was no one there. I stepped to the railing; no barge or boat.

Clamence was suddenly conscious that God was mocking him and audibly laughing. What Clamence was hearing, in the secret recesses of his mind, was an echo of that derisive laughter which is the divine response to the proud defiance of men.

> *The kings of the earth set themselves,*
>   *and the rulers take counsel together,*
>   *against the Lord and his anointed, saying,*
> *"Let us burst their bonds asunder,*
>   *and cast their cords from us."*
> *He who sits in the heavens laughs;*
>   *the Lord has them in derision* (Psalm 2:2, 3).

It was the mocking laughter of God which Clamence heard. It enabled him to gain a deeper insight into himself. He began to understand the extent to which pride had been the secret motivation of his life. "After prolonged research on myself, I brought out the fundamental duplicity of the human being. Then I realised, as a result of delving in my memory, that modesty helped me to shine, humility to conquer, and virtue to oppress. . . . Thus the surface of all my virtues," he admits, "had a less imposing reverse side."

It was this discovery of what he really was that led him to adopt the role of a "judge-penitent." He had an obsessive fear that he might die without having confessed all his lies. He was fearful of aggravating guilt by further lies. "Since I was a liar, I would reveal this and hurl my duplicity in the face of all those imbeciles, even before they discovered it." "I wanted to upset the game and above all to destroy that flattering reputation, the thought of which threw me into a rage." "I wanted to break open the handsome wax-figure I presented everywhere." To achieve this end he did outrageous things calculated to shock: "Courteously, with a solidarity charged with emotion, I used to spit daily in the face of all the blind."

These acts of calculated defiance were, of course, exhibitionistic. Clamence was haunted by the obsessive memory of his guilt. One day, travelling on the upper deck of an ocean liner, he saw, far off at sea, a black speck on the steel-grey ocean. He turned away at once and his heart began to beat wildly.

When I forced myself to look, the black speck had disappeared. I was on the point of shouting, of stupidly calling for help, when I saw it again. It was one of those bits of refuse that ships leave behind them. Yet I had not been able to endure watching it; for I had thought at once of a drowning person. Then I realized, calmly as you resign yourself to an idea the truth of which you have long known, that that cry which had sounded over the Seine behind me years before had never ceased, carried by the river to the waters of the Channel, to travel throughout the world, across the limitless expanse of the ocean, and that it had waited for me there until the day I had encountered it. I realized likewise that it would continue to await me on seas and rivers, everywhere, in short, where lies the bitter water of my baptism.[4]

On another occasion he was accompanying his friend home. He stopped when they reached a bridge. To his companion he explained: "I'll leave you near this bridge. I never cross a bridge at night. It's the result of a vow. Suppose, after all, that someone should jump in the water. One of two things — either you do likewise to fish him out and, in cold weather, you run a great risk! Or you forsake him there and suppressed dives sometimes leave one strangely aching."

Clamence discovered that there are no means known to man by which the past can be erased and the stain of guilt expunged. He thinks of religion "as a huge laundering venture," and even that, he immediately adds, "was once but briefly, for exactly three years, and it wasn't called religion." Since the time of Christ, he says bitterly, "soap has been lacking, our faces are dirty, and we wipe one another's noses." Guilt is a painful, palpable reality. We don't have to wait for the Last Judgment, he says; it takes place every day.

Camus' allegory is the story of a man who, having been a Pharisee, becomes a penitent. He seeks to perpetuate freedom by living in an honest and open confession of sin, in the hope that others will also be helped to saving self-awareness. "Covered with ashes, tearing my hair, my face, scarred by clawing, but with piercing eyes, I stand before all humanity recapitulating my shames without losing sight of the effect I am producing,

---

[4] *Ibid.*, p. 108.

and saying: 'I was the lowest of the low.' Then imperceptibly
I pass from the 'I' to the 'we'." Thus, "at the same time the
portrait I hold out to my contemporaries becomes a mirror."

For the Chaplain in *St. Joan* the scorching flames of the
fire were the instrument of his searing self-illumination; for
Jean-Baptiste Clamence, the lonely tragedy of the bridge; for
Willy Loman, in Arthur Miller's play *Death of a Salesman,*
the occasion of his calamitous exposure — the stripping of the
veil — was the unexpected visit of his son to a hotel in Boston.

Willy Loman, as portrayed by Arthur Miller, is a seedy
character. He is inordinately proud of his younger son, Biff,
in whose athletic achievements he finds some measure of
vicarious self-fulfillment. Biff, however, spends too much
time practising, and, as a result, gets poor grades. Biff is
accepted by the University of Virginia on condition of successful graduation from high school. His father is in Boston
when Biff learns that he has failed in mathematics. He rushes
to Boston to persuade his father to intercede with the head-
master. He is confident his Dad will be able to handle the
situation. He can trust his Dad. His Dad is a real pal. He
finds the hotel in Boston and immediately goes to his father's
room. He knocks eagerly and impatiently at the door. There
is a long wait. Inside, his father is entertaining a lady friend.
The woman says,

> Aren't you going to answer the door?
>
> WILLY: They're knocking on the wrong door.
>
> THE WOMAN: But I felt the knocking. And he heard us
> talking in here. Maybe the hotel's on fire!
>
> WILLY; *his terror rising*: It's a mistake.
>
> THE WOMAN: Then tell him to go away!
>
> WILLY: There's nobody there.
>
> THE WOMAN: It's getting on my nerves, Willy. There's
> somebody standing out there and it's getting on my nerves!
>
> WILLY, *pushing her away from him*: All right, stay in the
> bathroom here, and don't come out. I think there's a law
> in Massachusetts about it, so don't come out. It may be
> that new room clerk. He looked very mean. So don't
> come out. It's a mistake, there's no fire.
>
> *The knocking is heard again. He takes a few steps away
> from her, and she vanishes into the wing. The light follows*

him, and now he is facing young Biff, who carries a suitcase.
Biff steps toward him. The music is gone.

BIFF: Why didn't you answer?

WILLY: Biff! What are you doing in Boston?

BIFF: Why didn't you answer? I've been knocking for five
minutes, I called you on the 'phone —

WILLY: I just heard you. I was in the bathroom and had
the door shut. Did anything happen home?

BIFF: Dad — I let you down.

WILLY: What do you mean?

BIFF: Dad . . . .

WILLY: Biffo, what's this about? *Putting his arm around
Biff:* Come on, let's go downstairs and get you a malted.

BIFF: Dad, I flunked math.

WILLY: Not for the term?

BIFF: The term. I haven't got enough credits to graduate.

WILLY: You mean to say Bernard wouldn't give you the
answer?

BIFF: He did, he tried, but I only got a sixty-one.

WILLY: And they wouldn't give you four points?

BIFF: Birnbaum refused absolutely. I begged him, Pop, but
he won't give me those points. You gotta talk to him before they close the school. Because if he saw the kind of
man you are, and you just talked to him in your way, I'm
sure he'd come through for me. The class came right
before practice see, and I didn't go enough. Would you
talk to him? He'd like you, Pop. You know the way
you could talk.

WILLY: You're on. We'll drive right back.

BIFF: Oh, Dad, good work! I'm sure he'll change it for you!

WILLY: Go downstairs and tell the clerk I'm checking out.
Go right down.

BIFF: Yes, sir! See, the reason he hates me, Pop — one day
he was late for class so I got up at the blackboard and
imitated him. I crossed my eyes and talked with a lithp.

WILLY, *laughing:* You did? The kids like it?

BIFF: They nearly died laughing!

WILLY: Yeah? What'd you do?

BIFF: The thquare root of thixthy twee is . . .

Willy bursts out laughing; Biff joins him.

And in the middle of it he walked in!

Willy laughs and The Woman joins in offstage.

WILLY, *without hesitation*: Hurry downstairs and . . .

BIFF: Somebody in there?

WILLY: No, that was next door.

The Woman laughs offstage.

BIFF: Somebody got in your bathroom!

WILLY: No, it's the next room, there's a party —

The Woman enters, laughing. She lisps this: Can I come in? There's something in the bathtub, Willy, and it's moving!

Willy looks at Biff, who is staring open-mouthed and horrified at The Woman.

WILLY: Ah — you better go back to your room. They must be finished painting by now. They're painting her room so I let her take a shower here. Go back, go back. . . . *He pushes her.*

THE WOMAN, *resisting*: But I've got to get dressed, I can't —

WILLY: Get out of here! Go back, go back . . .

Suddenly striving for the ordinary: This is Miss Francis, Biff, she's a buyer. They're painting her room. Go back, Miss Francis, go back . . .

THE WOMAN: But my clothes, I can't go out naked in the hall!

WILLY, *pushing her offstage*: Get outa here! Go back, go back!

Biff slowly sits down on his suitcase as the argument continues offstage.

THE WOMAN: Where's my stockings? You promised me stockings, Willy!

WILLY: I have no stockings here!

THE WOMAN: You had two boxes of size nine sheers for me, and I want them!

WILLY: Here, for God's sake, will you get outa here!

THE WOMAN, *enters holding a box of stockings*: I just hope there's nobody in the hall. That's all I hope.

To Biff: Are you football or baseball?

BIFF: Football.

THE WOMAN, *angry, humiliated*: That's me too. G'night.
She snatches her clothes from Willy, and walks out.

WILLY, *after a pause*: Well, better get going. I want to
get to the school first thing in the morning. Get my suits
out of the closet. I'll get my valise. *Biff doesn't move.*
What's the matter? *Biff remains motionless, tears falling.*
She's a buyer. Buys for J. H. Simmons. She lives down
the hall — they're painting. You don't imagine . . .
He breaks off. After a pause: Now listen, pal, she's
just a buyer. She sees merchandise in her room and
they have to keep it looking just so . . . *Pause. Assuming
command*: All right, get my suits. *Biff doesn't move.*
Now stop crying and do as I say. I gave you an order.
Biff, I gave you an order! Is that what you do when
I give you an order? How dare you cry! *Putting his arm
around Biff*: Now look, Biff, when you grow up you'll
understand about these things. You mustn't — you mustn't
overemphasize a thing like this. I'll see Birnbaum first thing
in the morning.

BIFF: Never mind.

WILLY, *getting down beside Biff*: Never mind! He's going
to give you those points, I'll see to it.

BIFF: He wouldn't listen to you.

WILLY: He certainly will listen to me. You need those
points for the U. of Virginia.

BIFF: I'm not going there.

WILLY: Heh? If I can't get him to change that mark you'll
make it up in summer school. You've got all summer to —

BIFF, *his weeping breaking from him*: Dad . . .

WLLY, *infected by it*: Oh, my boy . . .

BIFF: Dad . . .

WILLY: She's nothing to me, Biff. I was lonely, I was terribly
lonely.

BIFF: You — you gave her Mama's stockings! *His tears
break through and he rises to go.*

WILLY, *grabbing for Biff*: I gave you an order!

BIFF: Don't touch me, you — liar!

WILLY: Apologize for that!

BIFF: You fake! You phony little fake! You fake!

*Overcome, he turns quickly and weeping fully goes out
with his suitcase. Willy is left on the floor on his knees.*

> WILLY: I gave you an order! Biff, come back here or I'll beat
> you! Come back here! I'll whip you![5]

For Biff, the revelation of his father's miserable duplicity is
the shattering of an idol. He cannot erase from his mind the
memory of his father's guilt. He goes to pieces. He ceases to
care. He becomes a drifter and a waster.

For Willy Loman, the consequences of that hour of naked
exposure before the horrified eyes of his incredulous son are
even more catastrophic. He finds himself loathed and despised,
spurned and rejected.

There is, associated with guilt, an awful indelibility:

> *The Moving Finger writes, and, having writ,*
> *Moves on: nor all thy Piety nor Wit*
> *Shall lure it back to cancel half a Line,*
> *Nor all thy Tears wash out a Word of it.*[6]

But there is hope beyond despair. God, the prophet Zechariah
says, has opened a fountain to cleanse from sin and uncleanness (Zechariah 13:1). God, according to the Christian Gospel, meets man's guilt with His grace, and cleanses and forgives
the penitent sinner.

The poet Cowper celebrates this saving truth:

> *There is a fountain filled with blood*
> *Drawn from Immanuel's veins,*
> *And sinners, plunged beneath that flood*
> *Lose all their guilty stains.*

[5] *Death of a Salesman* (Viking, New York, 1958), pp. 117-21.
[6] *Omar Khayyam* li.

Some Sweet Oblivious Antidote
or
the gift of pardon

On that day there shall be a fountain opened for the house of David and the inhabitants of Jerusalem to cleanse them from sin and uncleanness (Zechariah 13:1).

Graham Greene emphatically denies that his novel *The Quiet American* was written with a polemical intent. It was not meant to be, he insists, an attack on American foreign policy. It was written, he says, as a religious tract: as "a kind of morality about religion."[1]

Set in the context of the war in Indo-China, the story revolves around two men: Fowler, an English journalist, and Alden Pyle of the American Economic Mission. The men are perfect foils for one another: Fowler is a cynic who does not want to get involved, whereas Pyle is an innocent and an idealist. He wants to form a Third Force. Fowler goes out with a French patrol. By the time they return, their total bag of victims is a mother and a child who got themselves caught in the line of fire. The dead child haunts Fowler. When he plays dice the war comes back to him and he thinks of the dead child.

[1] *New York Times,* January 20, 1957, p. 8.

Pyle is restlessly anxious to do good (the title of the book is consciously ironic), but his profound ignorance of the political realities of the situation makes him an easy dupe for a secret underground organization which is, in fact, Communist. Fowler is aware that Pyle must be put out of the way. His well-intentioned but foolish activities are incredibly dangerous. Fowler knows that Pyle is ignorant of the harm he is doing. Pyle looks at the blood on his shoes, the freshly spattered blood of women and children killed by a bomb which he had planted, and he casually remarks: "I must get a shine before I see the Minister." In his blundering do-goodism, in his criminal ineptitude, he represents, in Graham Greene's gallery, "the graceless, sinless, empty chromium world."

Fowler does not want to be involved. He knows that each side is dirty. The human situation being what it is, let them fight, he says, let them love, let them murder. Heng, the wise old Chinese, tells Fowler: "Sooner or later one has to take sides. If one is to remain human."

Fowler is aware that he cannot get involved without getting his hands dirty. Nevertheless, he realizes he must act. He acquiesces in the assassination of Pyle and thereby frustrates the activities of the underground. As a result, he gets his hands dirty. He knows that he needs absolution and forgiveness. "If only," he says unhappily, "there was someone to whom I could say I was sorry."

It is not possible to be human alone. And the price of participation is being implicated in the sin of the world. "Everyone of one," Dostoevsky declares, "is undoubtedly responsible for all men and everything on earth, not merely through the general sinfulness of creation, but each one personally for all mankind and every individual man."[2] That is why every man needs forgiveness. Kafka asks: Is there someone who wants to help? Who is it? Is it a friend? A good man? Someone who sympathizes? Is it an individual? Is it everybody? Is there still help? Fowler echoes the same prayer: "If only there was someone to whom I could say I was sorry."

James Boswell, in his inimitable way, tells a touching story

2 *The Brothers Karamazov*, p. 200.

of Dr. Johnson's childhood. When Samuel was a boy, his father kept a stall on market days in Uttoxeter. One day he asked Samuel to look after it. The proud and sensitive boy refused. He never forgave himself for his act of stubborn defiance. Years later, after his father's death, he made his way to Uttoxeter and, for two hours, stood bareheaded in the rain, standing on the very spot where his father's stall had once stood. It was a vain and pathetic attempt to salve (in Dr. Johnson's own words) a secret discontent.[3]

In the heart of every man there is a hunger for forgiveness. It is tempting to think that forgiveness can be won by the simple expedient of voluntarily accepting punishment. Oedipus, after discovering that he has been guilty of the crime of parricide and incest (though unwittingly), puts out his eyes, exclaiming:

> O Light! May I never look on you again,
> Revealed as I am, sinful in my begetting,
> Sinful in marriage, sinful in shedding blood!

He destroys his eyes so that they

> . . . should see no longer his shame, his guilt,
> No longer see that they should never have seen,
> Nor see, unseeing, those he had longed to see
> Henceforth seeing nothing but night. . . .[4]

Likewise, Othello, after the murder of the lovely Desdemona, regards self-destruction as the only honorable way left open to him. He passes judgment on himself, crying, "No way but this," as he stabs himself.

"A large part of modern man's masochism and darkly enjoyed self-torture," says Roland Mushat Frye, "is but a form of the perennial attempt to punish himself because of his own desperate and largely unconscious feelings of guilt."[5] As children, "we misbehaved," Harry explains, in *The Family Reunion,*

---

[3] Hesketh Pearson, *Johnson and Boswell* (Heinemann, London, 1958), p. 13.

[4] Sophocles, *King Oedipus.*

[5] *Perspective on Man* (Westminster, Philadelphia, 1961), p. 115.

in order to be punished,
For punishment made us feel less guilty.[6]

In Bernard Shaw's comedy *Major Barbara,* we have an amusing illustration of the lengths to which a man will go in a desperate endeavor to regain peace of mind and to achieve a quiet conscience. Bill Walker is a Cockney whose girl friend, Mog, has been converted and has joined the Salvation Army. Bill, infuriated, goes to the hostel to get her back. He finds his way blocked by Jenny Hill, the Salvation Army girl on duty. Bill, who has been drinking, is truculent.

> BILL. I know you. Youre the one that took way my girl. Youre the one that set er agen me. Well, I'm goin to av er out. Not that I care a curse for her or you: see? But I'll let er know; and I'll let you know. I'm goin to give er a doin thatll teach er to cut away from me. Now in with you and tell er to come out afore I come in and kick er out. Tell er Bill Walker wants er. She'll know what that means; and if she keeps me waitin itll be worse. You stop to jaw back at me; and I'll start on you: d'ye hear? Theres your way. In you go. (*He takes her by the arm and slings her towards the door of the shelter. She falls on her hands and knees.*)[7]

One of the clients endeavors to intervene, but is violently struck. Jenny expostulates:

> Oh God forgive you! How could you strike an old woman like that?
>
> BILL (*seizing her by the hair so violently that she also screams, and tearing her away from the old woman*). You Gawd forgive me again and I'll Gawd forgive you one on the jaw thatll stop you prayin for a week. Now are you goin to fetch out Mog Habbijam; or am I to knock your face off you and fetch her myself?
>
> JENNY (*writhing in his grasp*). Oh please someone go in and tell Major Barbara — (*she screams again as he wrenches her head down*).
>
> BILL. You want to go in and tell your Major of me, do you?
>
> JENNY (*writhing in his grasp*). Oh please someone go in and

[6] T. S. Eliot, *The Family Reunion* (*The Complete Poems and Plays, 1909-1950*), p. 259.

[7] *John Bull's Other Island and Major Barbara* (Archibald Constable, London, 1907), p. 218.

BILL. Do you or dont you? (*She stifles a scream*). Yes or no.

JENNY. God give me strength —

BILL (*striking her with his fist in the face*). Go and shew her that, and tell her if she wants one like it to come and interfere with me. (*Jenny, crying with pain, goes into the shed.*)

With returning sobriety, Bill is penitent and ashamed. When Major Barbara confronts him he is guiltily defensive. She skillfully succeeds in further inflaming his awakened conscience. Almost crying, he protests:

> Why dont you lea me alown? Wot av I done to you? I aint smashed your face, av I?
>
> BARBARA (*softly: wooing his soul*). It's not me thats getting at you, Bill.
>
> BILL. Who else is it?
>
> BARBARA. Somebody that doesnt intend you to smash women's faces, I suppose. Somebody or something that wants to make a man of you.
>
> BILL (*blustering*). Make a man o me! Aint I a man? eh? aint I a man? Who sez I'm not a man?
>
> BARBARA. Theres a man in you somewhere, I suppose. But why did he let you hit poor little Jenny Hill? That wasnt very manly of him, was it?
>
> BILL (*tormented*). Av done with it, I tell you. Chack it. I'm sick of your Jenny Ill and er silly little face.
>
> BARBARA. Then why do you keep thinking about it? Why does it keep coming up against you in your mind? Youre not getting converted, are you?
>
> BILL (*with conviction*). Not me. Not likely. Not arf.
>
> BARBARA. Thats right, Bill. Hold out against it. Put out your strength. Don't lets get you cheap. Todger Fairmile said he wrestled for three nights against his salvation harder than he ever wrestled with the Jap at the music hall. He gave in to the Jap when his arm was going to break. But he didn't give in to his salvation until his heart was going to break. Perhaps youll escape that. You havnt any heart, have you?
>
> BILL. Wot d'ye mean? Wy aint I got a art the same as ennybody else?

BARBARA. A man with a heart wouldnt have bashed poor little Jenny's face, would he?

BILL (*almost crying*). Ow, will you lea me alown? Av I ever offered to meddle with you, that you come naggin and provowkin me lawk this?[8]

To purge his guilt Bill says that he will go and spit in the eye of Todger Fairmile, the converted wrestling and boxing champion, in the confident assurance that Todger will beat him badly. That will make things square. That will purge his conscience.

I'm goin to Kennintahn, to spit in Todger Fairmile's eye. I bashed Jenny Ill's face; and now I'll get me own face bashed and come back and shew it to er. E'll it me ardern I it er. Thatll make us square.

To Adolphus Cusins, a Professor of Greek, who is courting Barbara, Bill says:

Is that fair or is it not? Youre a gentmn: you oughter know.

BARBARA. Two black eyes wont make one white one, Bill.

BILL. I didnt ast you. Cawnt you never keep your mahth shut? I ast the gentmn.

CUSINS (*reflectively*). Yes: I think youre right, Mr. Walker. Yes: I should do it. It's curious: it's exactly what an ancient Greek would have done.

BARBARA. But what good will it do?

CUSINS. Well, it will give Mr. Fairmile some exercise; and it will satisfy Mr. Walker's soul.[9]

Bill's desire for punishment is frustrated by Todger Fairmile's refusal to retaliate. Bill returns to the hostel.

BARBARA. Hullo, Bill! Back already!

BILL (*nagging at her*). Bin talkin ever sence, av you?

BARBARA. Pretty nearly. Well, has Todger paid you out for poor Jenny's jaw?

BILL. No he aint.

BARBARA. I thought your jacket looked a bit snowy.

[8] *Ibid.,* pp. 228-9.
[9] *Ibid.,* p. 230.

BILL. So it is snowy. You want to know where the snow come from, dont you?

BARBARA. Yes.

BILL. Well, it come from off the ground in Parkinses Corner in Kennintahn. It got rubbed off be my shoulders: see?

BARBARA. Pity you didnt rub some off with your knees, Bill! That would have done you a lot of good.

BILL (*with sour mirthless humor*). I was saving another man's knees at the time. E was kneelin on my ed, so e was.

JENNY. Who was kneeling on your head?

BILL. Todger was. E was prayin for me: prayin comfortable with me as a carpet. So was Mog. So was the ole bloom-in meeting. Mog she sez "O Lord break is stubborn spirit; but dont urt is dear art." That was wot she said. "Dont urt is dear art"! An er bloke — thirteen stun four! — kneeling wiv all is weight on me. Funny, aint it?

JENNY. Oh no. We're so sorry, Mr. Walker.

BARBARA (*enjoying it frankly*). Nonsense! of course it's funny. Served you right, Bill! You must have done something to him first.

BILL (*doggedly*). I did wot I said I'd do. I spit in is eye. E looks up at the sky and sez, "O that I should be fahnd worthy to be spit upon for the gospel's sake!" e sez; an Mog sez "Glory Allelloolier!"; an then e called me Brother, an dahned me as if I was a kid and e was me mother washin me a setterda nawt. I adnt just no show wiv im at all. Arf the street prayed; an the tother arf larfed fit to split theirselves. (*To Barbara*). There! are you settisfawd nah?[10]

Jenny interjects: "I'm so sorry, Mr. Walker." Bill turns on her furiously:

I dont want to be forgive be you, or be ennybody. Wot I did I'll pay for. I tried to get me own jawr broke to settis-faw you —

JENNY (*distressed*). Oh no —

BILL (*impatiently*). Tell y'I did: cawnt you listen to wots bein told you? All I got be it was bein made a sight of in the public street for me pains. Well, if I cawnt settisfaw you one way, I can another. Listen ere! I ad two quid

saved agen the frost; and Ive a pahnd of it left. A mate
o mine last week ad words with the judy e's goin to marry.
E give er wot-for; an e's bin fined fifteen bob. E ad a
right to it er because they was goin to be married; but I
adnt no right to it you; so put anather fawv bob on an call
it a pahnd's worth. (*He produces a sovereign.*) Eres the
money. Take it; and lets av no more o your forgivin an
prayin and your Major jawrin me. Let wot I done be done
and paid for; and let there be a end of it.[11]

Jenny Hill replies that she couldn't possibly take the money.
Bill tries again; it's on his conscience, he says; he wants the
thing settled and finished.

It's this Christian game o yours that I wont av played agen
me: this bloomin forgivin an naggin an jawrin that makes a
man that sore that iz lawf's a burdn to im. I wont av it,
I tell you; so take your money and stop throwin your silly
bashed face hup agen me.[12]

"Nothing is more characteristic of the human sense of guilt
than its *indelibility*," says A. E. Taylor truly, "its power of
asserting itself with unabated poignancy in spite of all lapse
of time and all changes in the self and its environment. It is
only a man with the 'mentality' of the animal," he says bluntly,
"who can reconcile himself to the comfortable view that what
he has done amiss is 'washed off' by punishment, or 'made good'
by subsequent better conduct, and so no longer any present
concern of his life." The past, he adds, is not "dead"; it can
never, in this life, be buried and done with.[13] T. S. Eliot says
the same thing: the past, he says is

painful, because everything is irrevocable,
Because the past is irremediable,
Because the future can only be built
Upon the real past.[14]

It is this truth which the hedonist seeks to deny. To the
hedonist there is something morbid about preoccupation with

[11] *Ibid.,* p. 241.
[12] *Ibid.,* p. 242.
[13] *The Faith of a Moralist* (Macmillan, London, 1951), Vol. I, p. 174.
[14] *The Family Reunion* (*The Complete Poems and Plays 1909-1950*),
p. 228.

the past, and something foolish about an anxious concern over the future; the only thing that matters is present enjoyment. Omar, in a famous quatrain of the *Rubaiyat,* writes:

> *Ah, fill the Cup: — what boots it to repeat*
> *How Time is slipping underneath our Feet:*
> > *Unborn TOMORROW and dead YESTERDAY,*
> *Why fret about them if TODAY be sweet!*

Rabbi ben Ezra refutes him:

> *Thou to whom fools propound,*
> *When the wine makes its round,*
> *Since life fleets, all is change; the Past gone,*
> > *seize Today!*
> *Fool! all that is, at all,*
> *Lasts ever, past recall;*
> *Earth changes, but thy soul and God stand sure.*[15]

   In Shakespeare's tragedy, Lady Macbeth discovers that the past is not dead.   Burdened with an intolerable weight of guilt, restless and sleepless, she paces to and fro in the early hours of the morning.   Obsessively and compulsively she rubs her hands and cries out: "Out, damned spot! out, I say!   One, two; Why then, 'tis time to do it: Hell is murky! . . . . Yet who would have thought the old man to have so much blood in him? . . .   Here's the smell of the blood still!   All the perfumes of Arabia will not sweeten this little hand.   Oh!   Oh!   Oh!"   Her husband, who watches the scene, interrogates the doctor:

> *Canst thou not minister to a mind diseased;*
> *Pluck from the memory a rooted sorrow;*
> *Raze out the written troubles of the brain;*
> *And, with some sweet oblivious antidote,*
> *Cleanse the stuff'd bosom of that perilous stuff*
> *Which weighs upon the heart?*

The doctor replies that there is no remedy known to man: "the patient must minister to himself."[16]
   "Every man," writes T. S. Eliot, "is ultimately responsible

---

15 Robert Browning, *Saul.*
16 *Macbeth,* Act V.

for his own salvation or damnation."[17]   Every man, he implies, must make the choice between pardon or perdition, heaven or hell.

This is the theme of William Faulkner's searing novel *Requiem for a Nun,* the successor of an earlier novel, *Sanctuary,* which describes Temple Drake's horrifying initiation into vice. Temple Drake is an attractive and vivacious society girl.   The daughter of a judge, she attends a fashionable finishing school. One Saturday afternoon, on the way to a baseball game, she gets off the train and goes out driving with an irresponsible playboy, Gowan Stevens.   He has been drinking heavily. They drive into the country looking for a moonshiner's still, but Gowan, in a state of drunken intoxication, wrecks the car. Temple is abducted by a twisted gangster.   During the following days of terror and repeated rape she is conscious, in spite of herself, of perverted pleasure.   The moments of dark horror, of terrified agony, are shot through with feelings of strange joy.   Finally, after a succession of nightmare experiences, she is rescued and returned to her father.

In the years that follow she is tortured and tormented by the memory of her own awful guilt.   Faulkner relates the sequel in *Requiem for a Nun.*   Eight years have now elapsed. Temple is married to Gowan Stevens.   Gowan decided that the only decent thing that he could do, by way of reparation, was to marry the girl he had led into the gangster's path.   Their infant daughter is murdered by the Negro nurse, Nancy, a former dope addict and prostitute.   Nancy is duly sentenced to death.   The night before the execution Temple tries to obtain a last-minute reprieve from the Governor.   In an agony of remorse she confesses that Nancy's crime was motivated by a desire to prevent her from deserting her husband, whom she despises, and eloping with the gangster who had debauched her. She confesses that over the years she has been unable to erase the memory of her crime.   She says bitterly that she has not slept for six years.   Her lawyer replies: "The past is never dead.   It is not even past."   She is acutely aware that she is caught in the toils of her own soiled and sordid past.   "There's

[17] *Essays Ancient and Modern* (Faber & Faber, London, 1936), p. 119.

a corruption," she repeats, "even in looking at evil, even by accident. You can't haggle, traffic, with putrefaction." Temple knows that she is infected; she knows her own corruption, the reality of her guilt; and she is, she knows, doomed and damned.

The Negro murderess, by contrast, knows herself to be forgiven. She has accepted the gift of pardon. Nevertheless, she knows that she must accept the judicial consequences of her crime. When the death sentence is pronounced, she freely acknowledges the justice of the verdict, and humbly confesses: "Guilty, Lord."

Faulkner describes the final memorable scene. Temple, the mother of the murdered infant, is in the presence of Nancy, the convicted and condemned criminal. Temple is consumed with guilty remorse; Nancy is at peace with God. The accused has become the accuser. Nancy says that the last thing that a poor sinning man will abandon is the attempt to save himself. "Even with salvation lying right in his hand, and all he's got to do is choose between it; even with salvation already in his hand and all he needs is just to shut his fingers, old sin is still too strong for him, and sometimes before he even knows it, he has thrown salvation away just grabbing at hoping." Then, concerning her own awful crime, she says: "It's all right. I can get low for Jesus." Temple, conscious of the burden of her own intolerable guilt, cries: "Tell me what to do. . . . I'll do anything He wants if He'll just tell me what to do. . . . Let Him tell me how. How? Tomorrow, and tomorrow, and still tomorrow. How?" Nancy tells her how: "Trust in Him. . . . He will save you." And then, a little later, Temple cries: "Is there a heaven, Nancy?" and Nancy answers, "I don't know. I believes." The jailer returns. It is time for them to part. Nancy must be taken back to her cell to await the hangman's rope. Temple, in agonised desperation, cries out: "What about me? Even if there is one, and somebody waiting in it to forgive me, there's still tomorrow, and tomorrow." To this Nancy can only reply, "Believe." Nancy is taken away. Temple, as she leaves, asks desperately whether there is indeed Someone waiting to forgive, and she faces the awful alternative: "If there is no one, I'm sunk. We all are. Doomed. Damned." To which the lawyer replies: "Of course we are. Hasn't He been telling us that for going on two thousand years?"[18]

"What ails us," says P. T. Forsyth, "is not limitation but transgression, not poverty, but alienation. It is the breach of communion that is the trouble — the separation, the hostility." "As a race," he repeats, "we are not even stray sheep, or wandering prodigals merely; we are rebels with weapons in our hands."[19] What is required, to end the hostility, to overcome the separation, is unconditional surrender: the contrite confession of sin and the willing acceptance of forgiveness.

It is against the demand for repentance and the offer of forgiveness that the rational man most violently rebels. He will bear punishment; he will make restitution; but he will not, if he can help it, say that he is sorry. He prefers the proud and defiant Stoicism of Henley's well-known poem:

> In the fell clutch of circumstance,
> I have not winced nor cried aloud:
> Under the bludgeonings of chance
> My head is bloody, but unbowed.

> It matters not how strait the gate,
> How charged with punishments the scroll,
> I am the master of my fate:
> I am the captain of my soul.[20]

But there is a price to be paid. The price is the consciousness of unatoned sin. Raskolnikov, in Dostoevsky's novel *Crime and Punishment,* discovers that sin must be paid for. He adopts an attitude of bold defiance towards all the accepted conventions and sanctities of society. He scorns morality as an antiquated fiction. Moral judgments, he thinks, are a reflection of childish prejudices, a sign of contemptible weakness. They are, he insists, ridiculous and absurd; a man, to be strong and free, needs to emancipate himself from them.

To secure money and to test his theories Raskolnikov kills an old predatory usuress. "I wanted to know," he afterwards

[18] *Requiem for a Nun* (Penguin Books, Harmondsworth, Middx., 1960), pp. 235ff.

[19] *Positive Preaching and the Modern Mind* (Hodder & Stoughton, London, n.d.), pp. 55-6.

[20] W. E Henley, *Echoes,* iv. "Invictus." In Mem. R.T.H.B.

says, in discussing the matter, "whether I was like all of them, merely vermin, or a man; whether I was able to break through the barriers, or not — whether I would really stoop to gain power, or not; whether I was merely a trembling creature, or whether I had a right . . ." and so on. He commits the crime. No one sees him strike the blow. Nevertheless, he feels guilty. He tries to console himself by reflecting that after all she was only an old hag, one of a despised race, plying a disreputable trade. To Sonia he confesses: "I've only killed a louse, Sonia, a useless, loathsome, harmful creature." She replies: "A human being — a louse!" "I too know it wasn't a louse," he answers.

He finds that he cannot quiet his conscience. He never has an hour's quiet. He knows that he must talk, even to a friend who, as a detective, is engaged on the case. Again and again he visits his detective friend to discuss the case.

The police, baffled by the absence of clues, are unable to solve the murder. Raskolnikov could have escaped. But he is unable to keep silent. He feels under a compulsion to talk. He cannot bear to be alone. He wants to talk, to talk about those things that are most urgent to himself. When he speaks about them, he cannot hide his feelings, until at last, noticing how it gives him a little happiness even to speak about the case, and a little more happiness the more he seems to implicate himself, he one day goes the whole length, and first betrays himself, then confesses everything — and this to an accompaniment of moral happiness and ease so tumultuous and wonderful that he feels that he has never lived until this moment. When he confesses his guilt to his detective friend, the detective only replies, "I knew it all the time. The first day you came to see me, after the crime, I suspected you. When you began to speak of it, I became quite sure. I didn't lay hands upon you, for I knew that you were one of those who would have to come at last!"

The Psalmist testifies to a like experience:

> *When I declared not my sin, my body wasted away*
> *through my groaning all day long.*
> *For day and night thy hand was heavy upon me;*
> *my strength was dried up as by the heat*
> *of summer.*

When he confessed his sin he knew the inexpressible joy of sins forgiven.

> *I acknowledged my sin to thee,*
> *and I did not hide my iniquities;*
> *I said, "I will confess my transgressions to the Lord";*
> *then thou didst forgive the guilt of my sin*

(Psalm 32:3-5).

The Enigma of Death

or
the promise of immortality

If a man die, shall he live again? (Job 14:14).

An observing modern writer has said: "The fact of death is the great human repression, the universal 'complex.' Dying is the reality that man dare not face, and to escape which he summons all his resources. . . . Death is muffled up in illusions."[1] We do not need to cite Jessica Mitford's entertaining documentary, *The American Way of Death,* to substantiate the truth of this conclusion; the evidence is plain for all to see. It is reflected in the very language we use to describe the fact of death. There is an amusing incident in Noel Coward's comedy *This Happy Breed* which illustrates this. Frank and his sister Sylvia are sitting in the lounge room. Sylvia, who is a soured spinster, has become an ardent Christian Scientist. Frank and Sylvia have finished supper and are listening to the radio; Frank's wife Ethel is in the kitchen.

> SYLVIA: There's not so much to do since Mrs. Flint passed on.
> FRANK: I do wish you wouldn't talk like that, Sylvia, it sounds so soft.

[1] H. P. Lovell Cocks, *By Faith Alone* (James Clarke, London, 1943), p. 55.

SYLVIA: I don't know what you mean, I'm sure.

FRANK: (*firmly*) Mother died, see! First of all she got 'flu and that turned to pneumonia and the strain of that affected her heart, which was none too strong at the best of times, and she *died*. Nothing to do with passing on at all.

SYLVIA: How do you know?

FRANK (*firmly*): Mother died, see! First of all she got 'flu me down, see?

(*Ethel comes in*)

ETHEL: What are you shouting about?

FRANK: I admit it's only your new way of talking, but it gets explaining to Sylvia that mother died. She didn't pass on or pass over or pass out — she *died*.[2]

This conversation has a distinctly modern flavor. It reflects our self-consciousness, our uneasy embarrassment about the fact of death. In the judgment of Sylvia, Frank's bluntness is not only crude but coarse. Decency suggests that he should have used a gentle euphemism or a tactful circumlocution.

There has been a strange reversal, during recent years, in relation to what is the forbidden subject. Geoffrey Gorer points out that in the nineteenth century the processes of birth and reproduction were never mentioned in polite society, whereas the processes of death were an accepted subject of ordinary conversation. Today, by contrast, the processes of death are never mentioned in polite society, whereas the processes of birth and reproduction are a matter of compulsive preoccupation and anxious concern. In the prim and proper days of the nineteenth century, it was felt necessary, in the interests of morality and decency, modestly to drape the legs of tables and of chairs. Our grandparents, in their embarrassment and self-consciousness over the facts of birth, said that babies were found under gooseberry bushes, and we, in our self-consciousness over the facts of death, speak of "passing on."

This can be illustrated by reference to the field of literature. It is difficult to recall a play or a novel written during the past twenty-five years which has a "deathbed scene" in it, describing in detail the death of a major character from natural

2 Act 3, Scene 1.

causes.   Yet this topic was a set piece for most eminent
Victorian and Edwardian writers, and it evoked their finest
prose.   To create the maximum pathos or edification, they employed the most elaborate technical devices and supplied a
wealth of imaginative detail.[3]

A single example will suffice.   The climax to *The Old
Curiosity Shop* is the death of little Nell.   The book was published in serial form, and, when successive installments began
to foreshadow the death of the child, Charles Dickens was "in-
undated with imploring letters recommending poor little Nell
to mercy."   Dickens was acutely aware of the artistic demands
of the situation, and for days he was in a state of emotional
tension.   Dickens had to nerve himself to describe the death.
He confided, "All night I have been pursued by the child, and
this morning I am unrefreshed and miserable."   He felt the
suffering so intensely that he described it as "anguish unspeak-
able."   Writing to George Cattermole he said, "I am breaking
my heart over this story."

When the final installment was published, with the litho-
graph illustration showing the dead child lying on a bed with
pieces of holly on her breast, the resulting emotional excite-
ment was almost unprecedented.   Macready, the noted actor,
returning from the theatre, saw the print, and a cold chill ran
through his blood.   "I have never read printed words which
gave me so much pain," he noted in his diary.   "I could not
weep for some time.   Sensations, sufferings have returned to
me that are terrible to awaken."   Daniel O'Connell, the Irish
Member of Parliament, reading the book in a railway carriage,
was convulsed with sobs and groaned, "He should not have
killed her," and threw the book out the window.   Thomas
Carlyle was utterly overcome.   Waiting crowds on the pier in
New York harbor shouted to the passengers, "Is little Nell
dead?"   The news flashed across the United States and rough
and hardy pioneers dissolved in tears.   Lord Jeffrey, one ·of
Her Majesty's Judges, was found by a friend in the library of
his house, with his head bowed on the table.   When his friend
entered the room, she saw that his eyes were filled with tears.

[3] Geoffrey Gorer, "The Pornography of Death," *The Encounter,*
October, 1955.

"I had no idea that you had bad news or cause of grief," she said, "or I would not have come. Is anyone dead?" "Yes, indeed," he replied, "I'm a great goose to give myself away, but I couldn't help it. You'll be sorry to hear that little Nelly, Boz's little Nell, is dead."[4]

Without any certainty in the life to come, modern man finds the facts of natural death and physical decomposition too horrible to contemplate, let alone to discuss or describe. It is symptomatic of our present condition that one of the most flourishing sects in the world today is Christian Science, which denies the fact of physical death and which refuses to allow the word to be printed in the columns of the *Christian Science Monitor*.

Evelyn Waugh's novel *The Loved One* is a brilliant satire on the grotesque extravagances which accompany burial in southern California. Ruth Mulvey Harmer, in *The High Cost of Dying,* in a chapter in which she describes funeral parlors picturesquely as "turnstiles to eternity," writes:

> The body is no longer a corpse; it is the "departed", the "loved one", or even — with greater liveliness — "Mr. ....". And "Mr. ...." is no longer "laid out" for viewing; if he is not actually stretched out on a bed in a "reposing room", he is in the "slumber room" waiting to greet visitors, with his nails carefully manicured, the proper make-up applied, and perhaps holding a pipe or a book in a remarkably "natural" way. . . . Coffins have become caskets to hold a precious treasure. . . . More recently, they have become "couches" to banish further all thoughts of death.[5]

Sir Francis Hinsley, in Evelyn Waugh's satire, has committed suicide by hanging. In the embalming rooms of the Whispering Glades the touching-up process is completed. His friend muses on the nature of the transformation:

> *They told me, Francis Hinsley, they told me*
> *you were hung*
> *With red protruding eye-balls and black*
> *protruding tongue;*

[4] Edgar Johnson, *Charles Dickens, His Tragedy and Triumph* (Victor Gollancz, London, 1953), Vol. I, p. 304.

[5] *The High Cost of Dying* (Collier Books, New York, 1963), p. 19.

> *I wept as I remembered how often you and I*
> *Had laughed about Los Angeles and now 'tis*
>   *here you'll lie;*
> *Here pickled in formaldehyde and painted like*
>   *a whore,*
> *Shrimp-pink incorruptible, not lost nor gone*
>   *before.*[6]

These are the lengths to which they go in the Whispering Glades of California to obliterate the evidences of self-inflicted death and to arrest the processes of physical decay: they preserve the body in formaldehyde. Arthur Koestler observes that "morticians endeavour to transform the dead, with lipstick and rouge, into horizontal members of a perennial cocktail party," and this horrid pantomime is due, he says, to the fact that there has been a flight from the tragic facts of existence.[7]

There is, in the sceptical and sophisticated world of today, a morbid fear of death and an anxious avoidance of everything associated with it. The consequences of this may be seen, for example, in the field of education. A number of American educationalists are busily engaged in revising nursery rhymes. No longer are the ears of children to be offended with deeds of violence and stories of sudden death: Grimm's Fairy Tales and the tales of Hans Andersen, all are being expurgated and revised. All references to evil and wickedness, to suffering and death, are being suppressed and expunged. Thus children will learn about the *Three Kind Mice* who

> *All ran after the farmer's wife,*
> *Who cut them some cheese with a carving knife.*
> *Did you ever hear such a tale in your life*
> *As three kind mice?*[8]

By an interesting coincidence it is the same school of educationalists who are chiefly concerned with disseminating and making known "the facts of life." No longer are children to

[6] *The Loved One* (Penguin Books, Harmondsworth, Middx., 1951), p. 69.

[7] *The Invisible Writing* (Beacon, Boston, 1955), p. 158.

[8] Joy Davidman, *Smoke on the Mountain* (Hodder & Stoughton, London, 1955), p. 74.

be threatened with complexes and laden with inhibitions; the facts of life are to be openly proclaimed. Tell the children all about the facts of life, but never tell them, they warn, about the facts of death.

This is the astonishing and anomalous situation in which we find ourselves: on the one hand, the facts of life openly proclaimed; on the other hand, the facts of death hidden, denied, ignored, and suppressed.

It has been pointed out, however, that what has been repressed in life has reappeared in the realm of make-believe, and that what has been rejected by our sensitive educationalists has been reaffirmed in the lurid pages of children's comic papers. Children, despite the protective precautions and elaborate suppressions of their elders, are exposed, in the realm of comic literature, to the glorification of crime and cruelty, lust and sadism, and the faked and fictitious presentation is far more horrifying than the reality that has been denied. Geoffrey Gorer insists that if men refuse to come to terms with the realities of life in an open and dignified fashion, then they must expect these realities to make themselves felt in other ways. "If we dislike the modern pornography of death," he writes, "then we must give back to death — natural death — its parade and publicity, readmit grief and mourning. If we make death unmentionable in polite society — 'not before the children' — we almost insure the continuation of the 'horror comic.' No censorship has ever been really effective."[9]

The fact remains that we live in the midst of a vast conspiracy of silence. "Death is muffled in illusions." Existentialism, however, points out that if we do not come to terms with death, we cannot come to terms with life. This is the theme of Sartre's short story *The Wall*. It is a discussion of man's capacity to stand up to torture and death. It is set in the context of the Spanish Civil War. Three Republican prisoners are in their cell on the night before their execution. Sartre describes their reactions during the tormenting hours of waiting, together with their humiliating bodily weaknesses and progressive demoralisation. Ibbieta, however, faces his fear

[9] *Identity and Anxiety* (Freedom Press of Glencoe, Illinois, 1960), p. 407.

and, by facing it, conquers it. He achieves a courage "on the other side of despair"; he faces death in a state of "horrible calm," without illusion.

This is what the generality of men are unable to do: they are unable to face death without illusion. Tolstoy makes this point with impressive power in his story *The Death of Ivan Illyich* (a work which William Barrett describes as "a basic scripture for existential thought").[10] Ivan Illyich refuses to face the fact that his illness is mortal. To all others the signs of death are already present. His wife, knowing his condition, persuades him to take Communion.

"My darling, do this for me . . . It cannot hurt and frequently it helps. Healthy people frequently do it."

He opened his eyes wide.

"What? Communion? What for? It is not necessary! Still —"

She burst out weeping.

"Yes, my dear? I will send for our priest — he is such a nice man."

"All right, very well," he muttered.

When the priest came and took his confession, he softened, seemed to feel a relief from his doubts, and so from his suffering, and for a moment was assailed by hope. . . .

When, after the communion, he was put down on the bed, he for a moment felt easier, and again there appeared hope of life. He began to think of the operation which had been proposed to him. "I want to live, to live", he said to himself. His wife came back to congratulate him; she said the customary words, and added, "Truly, are you not feeling better?"

Without looking at her, he said, "Yes".

Her attire, her figure, the expression of the face, the sound of her voice, everything told him one and the same thing: "It is not the right thing. Everything which you have lived by is a lie, a deception which conceals from you life and death." The moment he thought so, there arose his hatred, and with his hatred came physical, agonized sufferings, and

[10] "Existentialism as a Symptom of Man's Contemporary Crisis," in *Spiritual Problems in Contemporary Literature,* ed. S. R. Hopper (Harper, New York, 1957), p. 143.

with the sufferings the consciousness of inevitable, near perdition.[11]

It is time to analyze, in terms of greater particularity, the significance of death. What is it that gives to death its terror and its sting? An answer may be found in the painfully detailed account which Dostoevsky gives of his own confrontation with death. He was arrested, together with other members of a student reading circle, and charged with offences against the Russian censorship. On December 22, 1849, the forty-four accused were taken to the Semyonovsky drill ground. The sheriff read out the sentences. Again and again the fateful words were pronounced: "Sentenced to be shot!" Years later Dostoevsky used to hear them as he awoke in the night. The accused were forced to put on the white shirts of the condemned, and for more than twenty minutes they stood in the bitter Russian cold — fifty degrees below freezing-point. A priest invited them to make their confessions; only one did so. They all touched the crucifix with their lips, kissing it eagerly, hurriedly — just as though they were anxious to grasp something which might be useful to them afterwards. Dostoevsky kept thinking, and he actually said: "It is impossible. They can't mean to kill us." But his nearest companion pointed to a cart near the scaffold, with coffins covered with a large cloth.

About twenty paces from where he was standing were three posts. The first three prisoners were fastened to them with white caps drawn over their faces so that they could not see the rifles pointed at them. Then a group of soldiers took their stand opposite each post. Dostoevsky was the eighth, and therefore he would be among the third lot to go up. He had about five minutes to live, and those five minutes seemed to be a most interminable period, an enormous wealth of time; he seemed to be living, in those minutes, so many lives that there was no need as yet to think of the last moment. He divided up the time into parts — one for saying farewell to his friends, two minutes for that; then a couple more for thinking over his own life and all about himself; and another

[11] *The Death of Ivan Illyich* (Oxford University Press, London, 1935), p. 70.

minute for a last look around. He contrived to kiss the two who were nearest to him, and he thought of his brother Mikhail and his family. Then he embarked on those two minutes which he had allotted to looking into himself. He put it to himself, as quickly and as clearly as possible, that here he was, a living, thinking man, and that in three minutes he would be a nobody; or if somebody or something, then what and where? A little way off there stood a church, and its gilded spire glittered in the sun. He stared stubbornly at this spire and at the rays of light; he got the idea that they were his new nature and that in three minutes he would become one of them, somehow amalgamated with them.

But worst of all was this thought: "What should I do if I were not to die now?" Men not condemned to die esteem life far too lightly. "What if I were to return to life again? What an eternity of days, and all mine! How I should grudge and count up every minute of it, so as to waste not a single instant!" This thought became such a terrible burden upon his brain that he could not bear it, *and wished they would shoot him quickly and have done with it.* He just waited and waited.[12]

And yet there was a terrible fear. He felt feeble and helpless; there was a choking in his throat. He did not lose his wits, but he was absolutely powerless to move. Then, when the soldiers had actually loaded their rifles, there was a shouting and other noises, and an officer came galloping across the square, waving a white handkerchief . . . . He brought a gracious pardon from the Emperor. Dostoevsky's sentence was commuted to four years' imprisonment in Siberia and four years' service as a private soldier.

Then the cart was uncovered. It contained, not coffins, but convict uniforms. The sentence of death had been only a threat, a "lesson not to be forgotten." But one who had been blind-folded to be shot had gone mad, and never recovered. Not one escaped without lifelong injury to his nervous system. And the twenty minutes without coats in the fierce cold of a Russian December morning meant that some

[12] Cf. *The Idiot* (Dutton, New York, 1943), p. 60.

had their ears and toes frozen, and one got chronic inflammation of the lungs which later developed into tuberculosis.

Dostoevsky confessed that he had not lived as he thought he would live if he were to "return to life again." He did not keep careful account of his minutes when that "eternity of days" was returned to him, those riches of time, but wasted many a minute. A. E. Baker makes this illuminating comment:

> All his life he was the man for whom time had stood still, who had faced the ultimate brute fear, who knew, as André Malraux has expressed it, that if life is worth nothing, nothing is worth a life. Arthur Koestler was condemned to death by Franco's lot. He speaks of those about to die as "men without shadows, dismissed from the ranks of the mortals". Dostoevsky had shared "the most complete experience of freedom that can be granted a man". This was behind the ever-present concern that filled each of his books. He was always trying to distract his attention from the soldiers loading their rifles, by the sight of "the general human distress, the misery of life and death". Kierkegaard was enigmatically prophetic of Dostoevsky's literary achievement when he wrote: "I have determined to read the writings only of the men who were executed or were in danger in some other way".[13]

It was this traumatic experience, so shocking and so searing, that led Dostoevsky to conclude that the certainty of inescapable death and the uncertainty of what is to follow are the most dreadful anguish in the world.[14] The accuracy of this observation must now be further explored.

On the one hand it is true that all must die. Our destiny, like the destiny of all men, is six feet of ground. "Dying my death," says Heidegger, "is the one thing no-one else can do for me."[15] In the triumph of death all our proud pretensions are humbled and abased. Sir Walter Raleigh, in the last sentences of his unfinished *History of the World*, apostrophises the inexorable and triumphant power of death:

---

[13] *Prophets for a Day of Judgment* (Eyre & Spottiswoode, London, 1944), pp. 58-9.
[14] *The Idiot* (Dutton, New York, 1943), p. 19.
[15] W. Barrett, *Irrational Man* (Doubleday, New York, 1962), p. 225.

> O eloquent, just, and mighty Death! whom none could advise, thou hast persuaded; what none hath dared, thou hast done; and whom all the world hath flattered, thou only hast cast out of the world and despised. Thou hast drawne together all the far fetched greatness, all the pride, crueltie, and ambition of man, and covered it all over with these two narrow words: *Hic Jacet.*

All our swelling ambitions, all our aspirations and achievements, all our hopes and fears, find their grave at last in the experience of a common mortality.   Francis Thompson speaks of man who

> *. . . dogs the secret footsteps of the heavens,*
> *Sifts in his hands the stars, weighs them as gold dust,*
> *And yet, is successive unto nothing*
> *But patrimony of a little mould*
> *And entail of four planks.*[16]

Pascal is right: "The last act is tragic, however happy all the rest of the play is; at the last a little earth is thrown upon our head, and that is the end forever."[17]

The ignominious fact is that we all must die.   God's judgment concerning man is this: "You are dust, and to dust you shall return" (Genesis 3:19).

There is, however, not only the certainty of inescapable death; there is also the uncertainty of what is to follow.   It is this which fills our hearts with fear.   "He who pretends to face death without fear," Rousseau affirms, "is a liar."[18]   "No rational man," says Dr. Johnson, in his blunt affirmative way, "can die without uneasy apprehension."   The fear of death, he says, is so natural to man that all life is one long effort not to think about it.[19]   Epicurus wisely observes that "what men fear is not that death is annihilation but that it is not."   It is not the fact of death itself but the gnawing uncertainty of what lies beyond the grave.

[16] "An Anthem of Earth," *The Works of Francis Thompson* (Burns & Oates, London, 1937), Vol. II, p. 263.

[17] *Pensees,* No. 210 (Dutton, New York, 1931), p. 61.

[18] Quoted, R. W. Mackenna, *The Adventure of Death* (John Murray, London, 1931), p. 23.

[19] James Boswell, *The Life of Samuel Johnson* (Dutton, New York, 1927), Vol. II, p. 212.

The poet Yeats writes:

> *Nor dread, nor hope, attend*
> *A dying animal;*
> *A man awaits his end,*
> *Dreading and hoping all.*[20]

Hamlet speaks fearfully of that "undiscovered country from whose bourn no traveller returns," which "puzzles the will, and makes us rather bear those ills we have, than fly to others that we know not of." "Thus conscience," he adds unhappily, "doth make cowards of us all."[21] Dryden frankly confesses,

> *Death, in itself, is nothing; but we fear,*
> *To be we know not what, we know not where.*[22]

If we enquire, more closely, what it is of which men are afraid, we must reply that it is the thought of that which lies beyond the grave. There is, says T. S. Eliot, in the sombre, haunting words of the Chorus in *Murder in the Cathedral,*

> *. . . behind the face of Death the Judgement*
> *And behind the Judgement the Void, more horrid*
> *than active shapes of hell;*
> *Emptiness, absence, separation from God;*
> *The horror of the effortless journey, to the*
> *empty land*
> *Which is no land, only emptiness, absence, the Void,*
> *Where those who were men can no longer turn the mind*
> *To distraction, delusion, escape into dream, pretence,*
> *Where the soul is no longer deceived, for there are*
> *no objects, no tones,*
> *No colours, no forms to distract, to divert the soul*
> *From seeing itself, foully united forever,*
> *nothing with nothing,*
> *Not what we call death, but what beyond death*
> *is not death,*
> *We fear, we fear.*[23]

[20] W. B. Yeats "Death," *Collected Poems* (Macmillan, London, 1955), p. 264.
[21] Act III, Scene 1.
[22] *Aureng-Zebe* iv, i.
[23] *The Complete Poems and Plays 1909-1950* (Harcourt, Brace, New York, 1952), p. 210.

The Bible says: "It is appointed for men to die once, and after that comes judgment" (Hebrews 9:27). Brunner comments: "It is not the fact that men die . . . but that they die as they do, in fear and agóny, with the anxious uncertainty about that which lies on the other side of death, with a bad conscience and the fear of possible punishment."[24] Reinhold Niebuhr adds: "Nothing expresses the insecurity and anxiety of human existence more profoundly than the fact that the fear of extinction and the fear of judgment are compounded in the fear of death."[25]

The justice of this observation may be demonstrated by reference to the testimony of Samuel Johnson. He was tormented by the thought of possible damnation.

> JOHNSON: "I am afraid that I may be one of those who shall be damned" (looking dismally). DR. ADAMS: "What do you mean by damned?" JOHNSON (passionately and loudly): "Sent to Hell, Sir, and punished everlastingly." BOSWELL: "But may not a man attain to such a degree of hope as not to be uneasy from the fear of death?" JOHNSON: "A man may have such a degree of hope as to keep him quiet. You see I am not quiet, from the vehemence with which I talk; but I do not despair." MRS. ADAMS: "You seem, Sir, to forget the merits of our Redeemer." JOHNSON: "Madam, I do not forget the merits of my Redeemer; but my Redeemer has said that he will set some on his right hand and some on his left." He was in gloomy agitation, and said, "I'll have no more on't."[26]

This obsessive fear of eternal damnation alternated with another fear, even more awful, that of annihilation. Often, in fits of absence of mind to which he was liable, he would be heard muttering to himself the lines from Measure for Measure,

> Ay, but to die, and go we know not where;
> To lie in cold obstruction and to rot.[27]

[24] The Christian Doctrine of Creation and Redemption, Dogmatics (Lutterworth, London, 1952), Vol. II, p. 129.
[25] The Nature and Destiny of Man (Nisbet, London, 1943), Vol. II, p. 303.
[26] James Boswell, op. cit., Vol. II, p. 526.
[27] Act III, Scene 1.

On one occasion Miss Seward was rash enough to say to him that at least one fear of death was absurd, "the dread of annihilation, which is only a pleasing sleep without a dream," which Johnson violently denied, saying: "It is *neither pleasing, nor sleep.*"[28]

It is sin, the Apostle says, which gives to death its sting (1 Corinthians 15:56). It is the consciousness of guilt that makes a man afraid, the secret awareness of judgment to come. The Christian man, however, is able to face death with a quiet conscience and a sure hope: a quiet conscience, because he knows that his sins are pardoned and forgiven; a sure hope, because Jesus has risen again from the dead. By His death and resurrection, says the Apostle, Jesus has "abolished death and brought life and immortality to light through the gospel" (2 Timothy 1:10).

If we ask what this means in the life of the Christian man, we cannot do better than quote Bunyan's immortal description of the way in which Mr. Valiant-for-Truth passed through the river of death.

> Then said he, "I am going to my fathers, and though with great difficulty I am got hither, yet now I do not repent me of all the trouble I have been at to arrive where I am. My sword, I give to him that shall succeed me in my pilgrimage, and my courage and skill, to him that can get it. My marks and scars I carry with me, to be a witness for me that I have fought his battles who will now be my rewarder." When the day that he must go hence was come, many accompanied him to the river side, unto which as he went he said, "Death, where is thy sting?" And as he went down deeper he said, "Grave, where is thy victory?" So he passed over, and the trumpets sounded for him on the other side.[29]

The Christian man is able to face, calm and unafraid, the final reality of death. With Edward Wilson of Antarctica he can say: "Death has no terrors."[30] By contrast, the natural man, without God and therefore without hope, is uneasy and

---

[28] Quoted, W. J. Bate, *The Achievement of Samuel Johnson* (O. U. P., New York, 1961), p. 162.

[29] *The Pilgrim's Progress* (Henry Bohn, London, 1857), p. 463.

[30] Quoted, George Seaver, *Edward Wilson of the Antarctic* (John Murray, London, 1946), p. 294.

secretly afraid. "I am," Thomas Hobbes confessed, "about to take my last voyage — a great leap in the dark."[31]

In popular mythology death has always been portrayed as a hideous skeleton with empty eyesockets and a long inexorable finger summoning man, and refusing to be denied. In Lucerne there is a bridge known as the Bridge of Death. In every panel of the bridge there is a picture of death breaking into life. Death comes to the soldier, the statesman, the merchant, the beggar; he comes to all and he comes to each, he comes, a grisly apparition filling the heart with dismay.

Boris Pasternak, in his Nobel prize winning novel, *Doctor Zhivago,* refers to "the centuries of systematic work devoted to the solution of the enigma of death so that death itself may eventually be overcome."[32] For the Christian man death, however, is not an enigma but an enemy, an enemy whose power has been broken and whose sting has been removed. It is true that "the wages of sin is death," but it is also true that "the free gift of God is eternal life in Jesus Christ our Lord" (Romans 6:23). At the last day, when God's triumph is complete, death itself will be abolished: "And God will wipe away every tear from their eyes, and death shall be no more, neither shall there be mourning nor crying nor pain any more, for the former things have passed away" (Revelation 21:4).

The natural man knows nothing about this assurance of a blessed immortality. For him, as John Donne once said, "death is a bloody conflict, and no victory at last; a tempestuous sea, and no harbour at last; a slippery heighth and no footing; a desperate fall and no bottom."[33]

For the Christian man, by contrast, death is, in the words of Dietrich Bonhoeffer, "the supreme festival on the road to freedom":[34] an occasion for joyous thanksgiving and confident rejoicing.

It is impressive to note how often Christian martyrs have invoked the metaphor of marriage to describe what death

---

[31] J. Watkins, *Characteristic Anecdotes of Men of Learning and Genius* (London, 1808), *in loc.*

[32] *Doctor Zhivago* (Collins, London, 1958), p. 19.

[33] *The Sermons of John Donne* (New York, 1958), p. 233.

[34] *Letters and Papers from Prison* (Fontana, London, 1960), p. 163.

means. On the evening before his martyrdom, Bishop Nicolas Ridley, the English Reformer, invited his keeper's wife and others at the table to his marriage: "for, said he, tomorrow I must be married, and so showed himself to be as merry as ever he had been before."[35] Sir Thomas Herbert tells us that Charles I went forth to his execution with the gay exhilaration of a bridegroom going forth to meet his bride: "This is my second Marriage Day; I would be as trim today as may be; for before night I hope to be espoused to my blessed Jesus."[36]

Trevor Huddleston, author of *Naught for Your Comfort*, has edited a collection of letters, written by men on the eve of their execution at the hands of the Nazis, entitled *Dying We Live*. From his prison cell in Hamburg, Hermann Lange wrote a final farewell letter to his parents. It is a letter of jubilant expectation and joyous hope.

> When this letter comes to your hands, I shall no longer be among the living. The thing that has occupied our thoughts constantly for many months, never leaving them free, is now about to happen. If you ask me what state I am in, I can only answer: I am, first, in a joyous mood, and second, filled with great anticipation. As regards the first feeling, today means the end of all suffering and all earthly sorrow for me — and "God will wipe away every tear from your eyes". What consolation, what marvellous strength emanates from faith in Christ, who has preceded us in death. In Him, I have put my faith, and precisely today I have faith in Him more firmly than ever, and I shall not yet be confounded. As so often before, I should like now also to refer you once again to St. Paul. Look up the following passages: 1 Corinthians 15:43f., 55; Romans 14:8. In truth, look where you will — everywhere you will find jubilation over the grace that makes us children of God. What can befall a child of God? Of what, indeed, should I be afraid? On the contrary — rejoice, once more I say to you, rejoice. And as to the second feeling, this day brings the greatest hour of my life! Everything that till now I have done, struggled for, and accomplished has at bottom been directed to this one goal, whose barrier I shall penetrate today. "Eye hath

[35] J. Fox, *A Universal History of Christian Martyrdom* (London, 1848), p. 862.
[36] *The Trial of Charles I* (The Folio Society, London, 1959), p. 126.

not seen, nor ear heard, neither have entered into the heart of
man, the things which God hath prepared for them that love
Him" (1 Cor. 2:9). For me believing will become seeing,
hope will become possession, and I shall forever share in Him
who is love. Should I not, then, be filled with anticipation?
What is it all going to be like? The things that up to this
time I have been permitted to preach about, I shall now see!
There will be no more secrets nor tormenting puzzles. Today is the great day on which I return to the home of my
Father; how could I fail to be excited and full of anticipation?
And then I shall see once more all those who have been
near and dear to me here on earth!

From the very beginning I have put everything into the
hands of God, if now He demands this end of me — good,
His will be done.

Until we meet again above in the presence of the Father
of Light,

your joyful Hermann.[37]

That is the authentic Christian confidence: a sure and certain
hope of resurrection unto eternal life. T. S. Eliot likens the
way men die to the whimpering of a dying dog:

> *This is the way the world ends,*
> *This is the way the world ends,*
> *This is the way the world ends,*
> *Not with a bang but a whimper.*[38]

For the Christian man, however, the last word is not with the
grave but with God: that is why there is no whimpering and
no whining, no repining and no complaining. That is why
the Christian man is able to say, with the Shepherd Psalmist:
"Even though I walk through the valley of the shadow of death,
I fear no evil; for thou art with me" (Psalm 23:4), and that
is why the Apostle Paul is able to say: "For I am sure that
neither death, nor life . . . will be able to separate us from the
love of God in Christ Jesus our Lord" (Romans 8:38-9).

[37] *Dying We Live* (Fontana Books, London, 1958), pp. 89-90.
[38] "The Hollow Men," *The Complete Poems and Plays 1909-
1950* (Harcourt, Brace, New York, 1952), p. 59.

Good, Merry, Glad and Joyful Tidings

or

the ecstasy of joy

Look to him, and be radiant (Psalm 34:5)

"We can," says Livy gloomily, "neither cure nor endure our vices." "We know and approve the better," Ovid confesses, "and do the worse." "Men love their vices," Seneca testifies, "and hate them at the same time." In the ancient world, men were wearily conscious of the bondage of besetting sin. Epictetus makes the unhappy comment: "Caesar can give peace from war but he cannot give peace from sorrow."[1]

> *On that hard Pagan world disgust*
> *And secret loathing fell.*
> *Deep weariness and sated lust*
> *Made human life a hell.*

> *In his cool hall, with haggard eyes,*
> *The Roman noble lay;*
> *He drove abroad, in furious guise,*
> *Along the Appian way.*

[1] For these and other references see T. R. Glover, *The Conflict of Religions in the Early Roman Empire* (Methuen, London, 1920).

He made a feast, drank fierce and fast,
And crown'd his hair with flowers —
No easier nor no quicker pass'd
The impracticable hours.[2]

It was the aim of the philosophers, Cicero tells us, to free "men from those most cruel of tyrants, eternal terror and fear by day and by night." Men "were stretching out their hands in longing for the farther shore. The inextinguishable instinct of humanity," Virgil insists, "craves for a voice of revelation to solve the mystery of life and death." We are compelled to sail the seas of darkness and doubt on the frail "raft" of our understanding, Plato comments, "not without risk, as I admit, if a man cannot find some word of God which will more surely and safely carry him."

The ancient world was not only anxious to solve the perplexing mystery of life, according to Virgil, but also to solve the impenetrable mystery of death. Men were caught in the toils of a profound scepticism. Euripides writes:

If any far-off state there be
Dearer to life than mortality,
The hand of death hath hold thereof,
And mists are under and mists above.
The other life is a fountain sealed,
The depths below are unrevealed,
And we float on legends forever.[3]

Many of the inscriptions along the Appian way, "the queen of roads," reflect an attitude of fatalistic resignation: "An eternal home"; "In eternal sleep"; and sometimes there is the symbol of the inverted torch, the emblem of despair. Occasionally the mood of sullen despair is relieved by a touch of flippant and cocky bravado: "A cocktail, please, for you and me" (*Misce, bibe, da mihi*); but the general mood is one of hopelessness: "Baths, wine and lust ruin our constitutions, but they make life what it is, farewell, farewell."

There was no general belief in personal immortality; at the

[2] Matthew Arnold, *Obermann Once More.*
[3] *Hippolytus* (translated, Gilbert Murray), p. 50.

most a man might hope to survive, but only as a bloodless and attentuated and ghostly shade. G. Lowes Dickinson, speaking of *The Greek View of Life,* says: "The tenderest of their songs close with a sob; and it is an autumn wind that rustles in their bowers of spring."[4]

The Roman satirist Juvenal ridicules as absurd any belief in a future life: "That the spirits of the dead are anything, or that the other world is anything, not even children believe, unless those still in the nursery." Hadrian, more piously, addresses a pathetic, wistful little poem to his soul:

> *Odd little comrade, comfortable guest,*
> *Capricious, elfin puff of air,*
> *You're off? But where? And when you've left my*
>   *breast,*
> *Tense little traveller, pale and bare,*
> *Will you find anything to laugh at there?*[5]

Epicurus contemptuously dismisses the fears and superstitions of men. "There is nothing to fear in God," he boldly asserts, "there is nothing to feel in death." The generality of men, however, remained unconvinced. Lucretius, the interpreter of Epicurus, observes that men torment themselves with imaginary fears.

> Life is darkened by the fear of retribution for our misdeeds, a fear enormous in proportion to their enormity, and by the penalties imposed for crime — imprisonment and ghastly precipitation from Tarpeia's Crag, the lash, the block, the rack, the boiling pitch, the firebrand, and the branding iron. Even though these horrors are not physically present, yet the conscience-ridden mind in terrified anticipation torments itself with its own goads and whips. It does not see what term there can be to its suffering nor where its punishment can have an end. It is afraid that death may serve merely to intensify pain. So at length the life of misguided mortals becomes a Hell on earth.[6]

[4] *The Greek View of Life* (University of Michigan Press, 1958), p. 34.

[5] Geoffrey Household's translation.

[6] *On the Nature of the Universe,* Book III.

These dreadful anticipations, Lucretius believes, are the figments of a too lively imagination, but, for "misguided mortals" they are a constant preoccupation.

This enables us to understand something of the phenomenal appeal of the Mystery Religions with their confident assurance of cleansing and immortality. To those who were initiated they gave, Cicero declares, "not only good cause why men should live joyously but also a better hope in death." "For us alone," Aristophanes claims, "who have been intiated and lived piously there is sun and cheerful light." But these blessings were the jealous and secret possession of a privileged few.

For the ordinary man, by contrast, there was only "emptiness, absence, the void." With the coming of Christ, a new day dawned, made bright with hope and gladness. Weeping, says the Psalmist, may endure for a night, but joy comes in the morning (Psalm 30:5). By His appearing, says the Apostle Paul, He has "abolished death and brought life and immortality to light through the gospel" (2 Timothy 1:10). For those who believe, there is not only hope and joy but also deliverance from fear and failure. The Apostle Peter puts the matter with simple clarity: "You believe in him and rejoice with unutterable and exalted joy. As the outcome of your faith you obtain the salvation of your souls" (I Peter 1:8-9).

William Tyndale rightly says that Christianity is

> Good, mery,
> glad and joyfull tydings, that maketh a
> mannes hert glad, and maketh hym singe,
> dance and leepe for joy.[7]

The joy which Christ bestows is an abiding possession: "No one," Jesus says, "will take your joy from you" (John 16:22). It is also a future hope: "We rejoice," says the Apostle Paul, "in our hope of sharing the glory of God" (1 Thessalonians 5:16).

"God is our exceeding joy" (Psalm 43:4), in whose presence there is fullness of joy, and at whose right hand there are pleasures for evermore (Psalm 16:11). The ransomed of the Lord, says the prophet Isaiah, shall

---

7 Prologue to the New Testament, 1523.

come to Zion with singing;
everlasting joy shall be upon their heads;
they shall obtain joy and gladness,
and sorrow and sighing shall flee away
(Isaiah 51:11).

"Today," says Gabriel Marcel simply, in his *Journal Méta-physique,* "I experienced grace for the first time," and then he adds: "I have never felt such joy."[8]

A like testimony is to be found in Pascal's famous "Memorial." His "Divine Metamorphosis and miraculous transmutation" was accompanied by a sense of great joy. For some time Pascal had developed, according to his sister, Jacqueline, an increasing "aversion for the follies and amusements of the world." On the night of November 23, 1654, he was meditating on the seventeenth chapter of St. John's Gospel when he had an overwhelming experience of the grace and goodness of God in forgiveness and acceptance. It was as though time stood still (he meticulously timed it, it lasted two hours) during which period of time he was conscious of nothing save the mystical presence of God. Immediately afterwards, Pascal wrote a detailed record of his experience on a piece of paper, an account of which he afterwards transcribed on a piece of parchment. Both copies were found after his death, carefully secreted and hidden in the lining of his coat. (The parchment has been lost; the paper original survives among the Pascal MSS.)

The year of grace, 1654.
Monday, 23rd. November, Feast of S. Clement, Pope and Martyr,
and of others in the Martyrology
Vigil of S. Chrysogonus, Martyr, and others,
From about half-past ten in the evening until about half-
past twelve
FIRE
God of Abraham, God of Isaac, God of Jacob, not of the
philosophers and savants
Certitude. Certitude. Feeling. Joy. Peace
God of Jesus Christ.

---

[8] Quoted, Marjorie Grene, *Dreadful Freedom* (University of Chicago Press, Chicago, 1948), p. 128.

My God and Thy God
'Thy God shall be my God'
Forgetfulness of the world and of everything except God
He is to be found only in the ways taught in the Gospel
Grandeur of the human soul
Righteous Father, the world hath not known Thee, but I have
known Thee
Joy, joy, joy, tears of joy
I have fallen from Him
'They have forsaken Me, the Fountain of living waters'
My God, wilt Thou forsake me?
May I not fall from Him forever
This is life eternal, that they might know Thee, the only
true God, and Jesus Christ Whom Thou hast sent
Jesus Christ
Jesus Christ
I have fallen away: I have fled from Him, denied Him, crucified
Him
May I not fall from Him forever
We hold Him only by the ways taught in the Gospel
Renunciation total and sweet
Total submission to Jesus Christ and to my director
Eternally in Joy for a day's exercise on earth
I will not forget Thy word. Amen.

The consequences of this experience were at once apparent.
Pascal immediately wrote to his sister a letter of bubbling
happiness. His sister was slightly shocked by his exuberance
of joy, "by an effervescence," Ernest Mortimer comments
"which Port Royal did not encourage in its penitents. But
he had cause for joy; the prisoner leaps to lose his chains."[9]
In her reply (January 19, 1655), Jacqueline says that she is
delighted to find him so gay, "notwithstanding," she confesses,
"I do not know how M. de Saci adapts himself to so light-
hearted a penitent."

John Bunyan, in his immortal allegory, attributes to Christian the same experience of ecstatic jubilation. After manifold dangers and temptations Christian reaches the cross:

Now I saw in my dream that the highway, up which
Christian was to go, was fenced on either side with a wall,

[9] *Blaise Pascal* (Methuen, London, 1959), p. 126.

and that was called Salvation. Up this way therefore did burdened Christian run, but not without great difficulty, because of the load on his back.

He ran thus till he came at a place somewhat ascending, and upon that place stood a cross, and a little below in the bottom a sepulchre. So I saw in my dream, that just as Christian came up with the cross, his burden loosed from off his shoulders, and fell from his back, and began to tumble, and so continued to do till it came to the mouth of the sepulchre, where it fell in, and I saw it no more.

Then was Christian glad and lightsome, and said with a merry heart, He hath given me rest by his sorrow, and life by his death. Then he stood still awhile to look and wonder; for it was very surprising to him, that the sight of the cross should thus ease him of his burden . . . . Then Christian gave three leaps for joy, and went on singing:

> "Thus far did I come loaden with my sin,
> Nor could aught ease the grief that I was in,
> Till I came hither: what a place is this!
> Must here be the beginning of my bliss?
> Must here the burden fall from off my back?
> Must here the strings that bound it to me crack?
> Blest cross! blest sepulchre! blest rather be
> The Man that there was put to shame for me!"[10]

Freed from the burden of his sin, Christian is transported with joy. His newfound joy finds spontaneous expression in the glad ecstasy of singing and leaping.

William Booth, the founder of the Salvation Army, encouraged an uninhibited exuberance of feeling. According to reports, he encouraged his followers, if they felt so inclined, to leap and jump. Dr. Farmer, the eminent organist of Harrow was once, tradition relates, invited to adjudicate at a Salvation Army Festival.

His musical soul was offended both by the drummer and the man with the French horn. He appealed to the drummer not to hit the drum so hard, to which the beaming bandsman replied, "Oh, sir, I'm so happy, I could burst the blessed drum." When Dr. Farmer turned with a word of similar appeal to the man with the French horn the en-

10 *Pilgrim's Progress,* pp. 53-4.

thusiast held up the much-twisted instrument and said, "But, sir, I'm so full of joy, I want to blow this thing quite straight."[11]

Constance Chadwick vividly describes the kind of impact which was made upon the staid life of Oxford University by the extravagant exuberance of the first members of the Oxford Inter-Collegiate Christian Union. For these evangelicals faith was an intoxication: "they passed through Oxford in the nineties of the last century," it has been said, "as a company of the first Franciscans passed through an Italian market place, less an order than an ebullition."[12]

John Masefield, in his dramatic poem of the conversion of Saul Kane, the drunken poacher and boxer, admirably illustrates the indubitable truth that joy is the natural expression of an appropriated forgiveness.[13] It was after a night of rollicking riot and drunken intoxication that Saul Kane came to Christ. The human instrument of his conversion was a Quaker, Miss Bourne.

> There used to be a custom then,
> Miss Bourne, the Friend, went round at ten
> To all the pubs in all the place
> To bring the drunkard's soul to grace;
> Some sulked, of course, and some were stirred,
> But none gave her a dirty word.
> A tall pale woman, grey and bent,
> Folk said of her that she was sent.
> She wore Friend's clothes, and women smiled,
> But she'd a heart just like a child.
> She come to us near closing time
> When we were at some smutty rhyme,
> And I was mad and ripe for fun;
> I wouldn't a minded what I done,
> So when she come so prim and grey
> I pound the bar and sing, 'Hooray,
> Here's Quaker come to bless and kiss us,
> Come, have a gin and bitters, missus.

[11] W. E. Sangster, *These Things Abide* (Hodder & Stoughton, London, 1939), p. 136.
[12] *Temple Gairdner of Cairo* (S. P. C. K., London, 1930), p. 2.
[13] *The Everlasting Mercy* (Sidgwick & Jackson, London, 1936).

Or maybe Quaker girls so prim
Would rather start a bloody hymn.
Now, Dick, oblige. A hymn, you swine,
Pipe up the "Officer of the Line" ' . . .

The men, in their fuddled intoxication, were shocked into silence.

The men stood dumb as cattle are,
They grinned, but thought I'd gone too far;
There come a hush and no one break it,
They wondered how Miss Bourne would take it.
She up to me with black eyes wide,
She looked as though her spirit cried;
She took my tumbler from the bar
Beside where all the matches are
And poured it out upon the floor dust,
Among the fag-ends, spit and sawdust.

'Saul Kane', she said, 'when next you drink,
Do me the gentleness to think
That every drop of drink accursed
Makes Christ within you die of thirst,
That every dirty word you say
Is one more flint upon His way,
Another thorn about His head,
Another mock by where He tread,
Another nail, another cross.
All that you are is that Christ's loss.'

The words burnt into his calloused soul; he rushed headlong from the pub, his cheeks aflame, in an agony of awakened guilt.

Out into darkness, out to night,
My flaring heart gave plenty light,
So wild it was there was no knowing
Whether the clouds or stars were blowing;
Blown chimney pots and folk blown blind
And puddles glimmering like my mind,
And chinking glass from windows banging,
And inn signs swung like people hanging,
And in my heart the drink unpriced,
The burning cataracts of Christ.

Confronted with the inescapable Christ, he made the great
surrender, and the peace of God came flooding in.

> *I did not think, I did not strive,*
> *The deep peace burnt my me alive;*
> *The bolted door had broken in,*
> *I knew that I had done with sin.*
> *I knew that Christ had given me birth*
> *To brother all the souls on earth,*
> *And every bird and every beast*
> *Should share the crumbs broke at the feast.*

Then joy filled his waking soul:

> *O glory of the lighted mind*
> *How dead I'd been, how dumb, how blind.*
> *The station brook, to my new eyes,*
> *Was babbling out of Paradise;*
> *The waters rushing from the rain*
> *Were singing Christ has risen again.*
> *I thought all earthly creatures knelt*
> *From rapture of the joy I felt.*

Billy Bray had the same sensation of everything being made
new. "I remember this," he relates, "that everything looked
new to me, the fields, the cattle, the trees. I was like a new
man in a new world." Temple Gairdner, the morning after
his conversion, had an illuminated text affixed to his wall:
"Behold, I make all things new." To Saul Kane everything
in the old familiar landscape was irradiated with the glory of
God.

> *All earthly things that blessed morning*
> *Were everlasting joy and warning.*
> *The gate was Jesus' way made plain,*
> *The mole was Satan foiled again,*
> *Black blinded Satan snouting way*
> *Along the red of Adam's clay;*
> *The mist was error and damnation,*
> *The lane the road unto salvation,*
> *Out of the mist into the light;*
> *O blessed gift of inner sight.*
> *The past was faded like a dream;*
> *There come the jingling of a team,*
> *A ploughman's voice, a clink of chain,*
> *Slow hoofs, and harness under strain.*

Up the slow slope a team came bowing,
Old Callow at his autumn ploughing,
Old Callow, stooped above the hales,
Ploughing the stubble into wales;
His grave eyes looking straight ahead,
Shearing a long straight furrow red;
His plough-foot high to give it earth
To bring new food for men to birth.

Seeing Callow ploughing in the field, Saul Kane knew that he had discovered God's will for his life. He was conscious of an ineffable sense of joy.

I kneeled there in the muddy fallow,
I knew that Christ was there with Callow,
That Christ was standing there with me,
That Christ had taught me what to be,
That I should plough, and as I ploughed
My Saviour Christ would sing aloud,
And as I drove the clods apart
Christ would be ploughing in my heart,
Through rest-harrow and bitter roots,
Through all my bad life's rotten fruits.

The poem ends in a paean of praise.

O Christ who holds the open gate,
O Christ who drives the furrow straight,
O Christ, the plough, O Christ, the laughter
Of holy white birds flying after,

Lo, all my heart's field red and torn,
And Thou wilt bring the young green corn,
The young green corn divinely springing,
The young green corn forever singing;

And when the field is fresh and fair
Thy blessed feet shall glitter there.
And we will walk the weeded field,
And tell the golden harvest's yield,

The corn that makes the holy bread
By which the soul of man is fed,
The holy bread, the food unpriced,
Thy everlasting mercy, CHRIST.

As a final example of the joy which accompanies and follows conversion we may cite James Joyce, *A Portrait of the Artist as a Young Man*.   Under the thin disguise of fiction, Joyce describes his own conversion in the person of Stephen Dedalus.   A Religious Retreat is conducted at the Jesuit School at which Stephen is a boarder.   Under the fervent and terrifying preaching of the Missioner, Stephen's guilty conscience explodes like a magnetic mine.   He is deeply convicted; he seeks a church in which to make his confession. He cannot bring himself to face his own religious director.

> He knelt in the silent gloom and raised his eyes to the white crucifix suspended above him.   God could see that he was sorry.   He would tell all his sins.   His confession would be long, long.   Everybody in the chapel would know then what a sinner he had been.   Let them know.   It was true.   But God had promised to forgive him if he was sorry.   He clasped his hands and raised them towards the white form, praying with his darkened eyes, praying with all his trembling body, swaying his head to and fro like a lost creature, praying with whimpering lips.
>
> — Sorry!   Sorry!   O Sorry!
>
> The slide clicked back and his heart bounded in his breast. The face of an old priest was at the grating, averted from him, leaning upon a hand.   He made the sign of the cross and prayed of the priest to bless him for he had sinned. Then, bowing his head, he repeated the *Confiteor* in fright. At the words *my most grievous fault* he ceased, breathless.
>
> — How long is it since your last confession, my child?
>
> — A long time, father.
>
> — A month, my child?
>
> — Longer, father.
>
> — Three months, my child?
>
> — Longer, father.
>
> — Six months?
>
> — Eight months, father.
>
> He had begun.   The priest asked:
>
> — And what do you remember since that time?
>
> He began to confess his sins: masses missed, prayers not said, lies.
>
> — Anything else, my child?
>
> Sins of anger, envy of others, gluttony, vanity, disobedience.

— Anything else, my child?

There was no help. He murmured:

— I . . . committed sins of impurity, father.

The priest did not turn his head.

— With yourself, my child?

— And . . . with others.

— With women, my child?

— Yes, father.

— Were they married women, my child?

He did not know. His sins trickled from his lips, one by one, trickled in shameful drops from his soul festering and oozing like a sore, a squalid stream of vice. The last sins oozed forth, sluggish, filthy. There was no more to tell. He bowed his head, overcome.

The priest was silent. Then he asked:

— How old are you, my child?

— Sixteen, father.

The priest passed his hand several times over his face. Then, resting his forehead against his hand, he leaned towards the grating and, with eyes still averted, spoke slowly. His voice was weary and old.

— You are very young, my child, he said, and let me implore you to give up that sin. It is a terrible sin. It kills the body and it kills the soul. It is the cause of many crimes and misfortunes. Give it up, my child, for God's sake. It is dishonourable and unmanly. You cannot know where that wretched habit will lead you or where it will come against you. As long as you commit that sin, my poor child, you will never be worth one farthing to God. Pray to our mother Mary to help you. She will help you, my child. Pray to Our Blessed Lady when that sin comes into your mind. I am sure you will do that will you not? You repent of all those sins. I am sure you do. And you will promise God now that by His holy grace you will never offend Him any more by that wicked sin. You will make that solemn promise to God, will you not?

— Yes, father.

The old and weary voice fell like sweet rain upon his quaking parching heart. How sweet and sad!

— Do so, my poor child. The devil has led you astray. Drive him back to hell when he tempts you to dishonour your body in that way — the foul spirit who hates Our Lord. Promise God now that you will give up that sin, that wretched wretched sin.

> Blinded by his tears and by the light of God's merciful-
> ness he bent his head and heard the grave words of absolu-
> tion spoken and saw the priest's hand raised above him in
> token of forgiveness.
> — God bless you, my child. Pray for me.
> He knelt to say his penance, praying in a corner of the
> dark nave: and his prayers ascended to heaven from his
> purified heart like perfume streaming upwards from a
> heart of white rose.
> The muddy streets were gay. He strode homewards,
> conscious of an invisible grace pervading and making
> light his limbs. In spite of all he had done it. He had
> confessed and God had pardoned him. His soul was made
> fair and holy once more, holy and happy.[14]

As he hears the words of absolution he experiences cleansing
and forgiveness; he knows what it is to be both "holy and
happy."

Joy, as every Christian knows, is the soul's seal of pardon,
the kiss of God's acceptance. No wonder there are trans-
ports of joy. Richard Crashaw celebrates the subduing wonder
of being loved and accepted by God.

> *Happy soul, she shall discover*
> *What joy, what bliss,*
> *How many heavens at once it is,*
> *To have a God become her lover.*[15]

Francis of Assisi was in love with God ("I am in love with
a bride nobler, richer and fairer than you have ever seen").
He described his followers picturesquely as God's Troubadours
—*Les Jongleurs de Dieu*. He had no time for those who were
sad and melancholy; he wanted followers who were radiant
with joy. His winsome faith found fitting expression in his
exquisite *Canticle of the Sun*.

[14] *The Essential James Joyce* (Jonathan Cape, London, 1950), pp.
282-3. It is true that Joyce subsequently lapsed into agnosticism, re-
pudiating both Ireland and the Church. Nevertheless, this account is
plainly a transcript from life, and bears on it the hallmark of authenticity.

[15] *On a Prayer-Book sent to Mrs. M. R.*

Most High, Omnipotent, Good Lord,
Praise, glory and honour be given to Thee with one accord!

To Thee alone, Most High, does praise belong,
Yet none is worthy to make of Thee his song.

Be praised, my Lord, with all Thy works whate'er they be.
Our noble Brother Sun especially,
Whose brightness makes the light by which we see,
And he is fair and radiant, splendid and free,
A likeness and a type, Most High, of Thee.

Be praised, my Lord, for Sister Moon and every Star
That Thou hast formed to shine so clear from
heaven afar.

Be praised, my Lord, for Brother Wind and Air,
Breezes and clouds and weather foul or fair —
To every one that breathes Thou givest a share.

Be praised, my Lord, for Brother Fire, whose light
Thou madest to illuminate the night.
And he is fair and jolly and strong and bright.

Be praised, my Lord, for Sister Earth our Mother,
Who nourishes and gives us food and fodder,
And the green grass and flowers of every colour.

Be praised, my Lord, for those who for Thy love forgive,
Contented unavenged in quiet to live.
Blest those who in the way of peace are found —
By Thee, O Lord Most High, they shall be crowned!

Be praised, my Lord, for our Sister Bodily Death,
From whom none can escape that has drawn breath.
"Woe to those dying in mortal sin!" He saith.
Blest those who find that in Thy Holy Will
The second Death to them will bring no ill.

Praise ye and bless my Lord, and do Him service due,
With humblest thanks for all He has done for you.[16]

[16] Translated by F. C. Burkitt.

There is a striking contrast between this canticle and Bach's well-known hymn, "Jesu, Joy of Man's Desiring." Francis had a joyous sense of the kinship of all created things; Bach's worship is centered solely on Christ, as the object of all striving and the fount of all joy.

> *Jesu, joy of man's desiring,*
> *Holy wisdom, Love most bright,*
>
> *Drawn by Thee, our souls aspiring,*
> *Soar to uncreated light.*
>
> *Word of God, our flesh that fashioned,*
> *With the fire of life impassioned.*
>
> *Striving still to truth unknown,*
> *Soaring, dying round Thy throne.*
>
> *Through the way where Hope is guiding,*
> *Hark, what peaceful music rings.*
>
> *Where the flock in Thee confiding*
> *Drink of joy from deathless springs.*
>
> *Theirs is beauty's fairest pleasure,*
> *Theirs is wisdom's holiest treasure.*
>
> *Thou dost ever lead Thine own,*
> *In the love of joys unknown.*

"Eye hath not seen, nor ear heard, neither have entered into the heart of man, the things which God hath prepared for them that love Him" (1 Corinthians 2:9, A.V.). The joys of earth are only a faint foretaste of the joys of heaven, an adumbration of that greater glory which is yet to be. "Joy," says C. S. Lewis simply, "is the serious business of heaven."[17]

The greatest joy in life, according to Augustine, is that of a sinner's conversion. Seven centuries later, Eadmen, the biographer of Anselm, recalling the teaching of his master, declared that, in the hereafter, the joy of the blessed will be

---

[17] *Letters to Malcolm: Chiefly on Prayer* (Geoffrey Bles, London, 1963), p. 122.

magnified a million millionfold, as each shares and reflects and multiplies the joy of all the others, and there will be joy within and joy without, joy above and joy below, joy around and joy everywhere, the joy that God has prepared for them that love Him.[18]

[18] *De Beatitudine Caeleste*, Migne, clix, col. 599. E. W. Williamson, *An Anatomy of Christian Joy* (S. P. C. K., London, 1946), p. 13.

The Academy of Love

or

the dilemma of means

Do not be overcome by evil, but overcome evil with good
(Romans 12:21).

"The Lord hath done great things for us," says the Psalmist exultantly, "whereof we are glad" (Psalm 16:3, A.V.). The forgiven man has a glad awareness of God's goodness, and a consequent desire to make it known. "Out of the abundance of the heart," Jesus testifies, "the mouth speaks" (Matthew 12:34). Augustine affirms: "What I live by, I impart." Peter and John, being warned and threatened by the Council in Jerusalem, reply: "We cannot but speak of what we have seen and heard" (Acts 4:20). There were times when Jeremiah, in the bitterness of lonely rejection and heartless derision, was tempted to speak no more. He found his pusillanimous fears overborne by an inner compulsion that could not be denied:

> *If I say, "I will not mention him,*
> *or speak any more in his name,"*
> *there is in my heart as it were a burning fire*
> *shut up in my bones,*
> *and I am weary with holding it in,*
> *and I cannot*
>   (Jeremiah 20:9).

What is our reaction to be to those who churlishly and ungratefully refuse the invitation to the banquet of heavenly joy? This is love's dilemma. Are there, for the Christian man, limits to the compulsion of love, and, if so, what are they? What does Jesus mean when He says: "Compel them to come in" (Luke 14:23)? What does St. Paul mean when he says that he became all things to all men that by all means he might save some (1 Corinthians 9:22)?

The ethical problem may be stated in summary form: Do the ends justify the means, or must the means we use be consistent with the ends we serve? The followers of Machiavelli and Marx have consistently subordinated morality to expediency, arguing, with superficial cogency, that a success gained is a method justified. "Our morality," Lenin admits, "is entirely subordinated to the interests of the class struggle of the proletariat." "We repudiate all morality," he says again, "that is taken outside of human class concepts."[1] The Christian moralist, by contrast, vigorously repudiates this depreciation of morality, and insists that, as evil communications corrupt good manners, so evil methods corrupt good ends.

Christians, however, are not alone in insisting that bad means cannot achieve good ends. "The ends cannot justify the means," says Aldous Huxley emphatically, "for the simple and obvious reason that the means employed determine the nature of the ends produced."[2] Dean Inge points out that revolutions which begin with the cry that the poor have nothing to lose but their chains invariably end in iron tyranny and universal serfdom.[3] The rule is: "the more violence, the less revolution" (Barthélemy de Ligt). "A violent revolution," Aldous Huxley rightly observes, "cannot achieve anything except the inevitable results of violence."[4] "Secularism," Dean Inge repeats, "promises an earthly paradise at the end of a flowery path, and gives us a premature hell at the end of a way of blood."[5]

1 Lenin, *Selected Works* (International Publishers, New York, 1943), Vol. IX, p. 475.
2 *Ends and Means* (Chatta & Windus, London, 1940), p. 9.
3 *The Fall of Idols* (Putman, London, 1940), p. 84.
4 A. Huxley, *op. cit.,* p. 25.
5 *Talks in a Free Country* (Putnam, London, 1942), p. 27.

Hegel makes the cynical observation that history teaches that "peoples and governments have never learned anything from history."[6] According to the popular aphorism, "those who do not study history are doomed to repeat it." There is justification for Gibbon's depressing conclusion that "history is little more than the register of the crimes, follies and misfortunes of mankind."[7]

It is not difficult to validate the truth of these sayings. Down the ages men have continued to seek peace by engaging in war, despite Christ's emphatic warning that "all who take the sword will perish by the sword" (Matthew 26:52). "The one thing that you cannot do with bayonets," a nineteenth-century master of the art of *realpolitik* said, "is to sit on them." "The truth seems to be," Arnold Toynbee comments, "that a sword which has once drunk blood cannot be permanently restrained from drinking blood again anymore than a tiger which has once tasted human flesh can be prevented from becoming a man-eater from that time onwards."[8]

Experience, it has been said, is a good teacher, but her fees are terribly high. Again and again mankind has been compelled to learn the bitter lesson, through acrid tears of pain, that "there is a way which seems right to a man, but its end is the way to death" (Proverbs 16:25).

Only a good tree, according to Jesus, can bring forth good fruit; an evil tree, He insists, brings forth evil fruit (Matthew 7:17). Nevertheless, men willfully and perversely persist in doing evil that good may come, despite the fact that all the evidence which we possess combines to demonstrate the bankruptcy of such a proceeding. Men forget that evil has a deadly power of recoil, and that those who resort to it always do so to their own hurt.

"The Christian Church itself," says Herbert Butterfield, in a memorable passage, "regarded as a visible and terrestrial institution, has not been exempt from that bias, that curious twist in events, that gravitational pull in human nature, which draws the highest things downward, mixes them with earth,

---

[6] *Lectures on the Philosophy of History,* Introduction.

[7] *The Decline and Fall of the Roman Empire,* chapter 3.

[8] *A Study of History,* D. C. Somervell's abridgment (Oxford University Press, London, 1946), p. 535.

and taints them with human cupidity."[9]   In nothing is this more apparent than in relation to the Church's use of means. The shameful truth is that, again and again, Jesus has been betrayed by those of His own household. "The Papacy" according to Thomas Hobbes, "is not other than the Ghost of the deceased Roman Empire, sitting crowned upon the grave thereof,"[10] and has shed, as the historian Lecky estimated, more innocent blood than any other institution in human history.   It is an alarming fact that "the devil frequently captures the organizations which were formed to defeat him, and uses them for his own purposes."[11]

And yet these calamitous betrayals would not have taken place had the Church been more attentive to the example of her Master.   At the beginning of His public ministry, Jesus was tempted in three ways to abandon the costly path of obedience for the convenient way of compromise and accommodation.   It is a depressing commentary on the life of the institutional Church that it has been so ready to accept the temptations which Jesus rejected.   This is the gravamen of Dostoevsky's impassioned indictment of the Roman Church in the prose-poem, "The Grand Inquisitor" (in *The Brothers Karamazov*).   A reconsideration of Christ's temptations in the wilderness, by those who profess to be disciples in the academy of love, is long overdue.

"The tempter came and said to him, 'If you are the Son of God, command these stones to become loaves of bread'" (Matthew 4:3).   In popular Jewish thought the Messianic age was depicted as a time of abundant material prosperity, "a feast of fat things, a feast of wine on the lees, of fat things full of marrow, of wine on the lees well refined" (Isaiah 25:6). It was not hard for the devil to suggest that this was the approved way in which to win men, foreshadowed in the prophecies of the Messiah.   On one occasion Jesus did indeed feed five thousand men with bread, and the result was that they immediately sought to take Him by force to make Him

---

[9] *Christianity and History* (G. Bell & Sons, London, 1950), p. 39.

[10] *Leviathan,* Part IV, ch. 47.

[11] W. R. Inge, *Assessments and Anticipations* (Cassell, London, 1929), p. 59.

King. Jesus was not deceived. He understood only too well the empty significance of their patronage: "Truly, truly, I say to you, you seek mé, not because you saw signs, but because you ate your fill of the loaves" (John 6:26). That was the unpalatable truth: He knew that they were seeking Him, not because He was the Son of God, but because He had given them bread to eat.

It is not a bad thing to give the hungry bread to eat; on the contrary it is, Jesus says, a blessed thing (Matthew 25:31-46). Unhappily, the agents of charity have often been tempted to use the exercise of charity as an opportunity for religious exploitation and sectarian advantage. Jesus, "moved by compassion," and by compassion alone, fed the multitudes; He would not prostitute the gift of bread by degrading the gift into a bribe.

George Orwell, in his searing autobiography, *Down and Out in Paris and in London,* speaks bitterly of this kind of purchased piety. He relates how a friend took him

> to a small tin-roofed shed in a sidestreet, rather like a village cricket pavilion. About twenty-five other tramps were waiting. A few of them were dirty old habitual vagabonds, the majority decent-looking lads from the north, probably miners or cotton operatives out of work. Presently the door opened and a lady in a blue silk dress, wearing gold spectacles and crucifix, welcomed us in. Inside were thirty or forty hard chairs, a harmonium, and a very gory lithograph of the Crucifixion.
>
> Uncomfortably we took off our caps and sat down. The lady handed out the tea and while we ate and drank she moved to and fro, talking benignly. She talked upon religious subjects — about Jesus Christ always having a soft spot for poor rough men like us, and about how quickly the time passed when you were in church, and what a difference it made to a man on the road if he said his prayers regularly. We hated it. We sat against the wall fingering our caps (a tramp feels indecently exposed with his cap off), and turning pink trying to mumble something when the lady addressed us . . . .
>
> Tea ended, and I saw the tramps looking furtively at one another. An unspoken thought was running from man to man — could we possibly make off before the prayers started? Someone stirred in his chair — not getting up

actually, but with just a glance at the door, as though half
suggesting the idea of departure. The lady quelled him with
one look. She said in a more benign tone than ever:
"I don't think you need go *quite* yet. The casual ward
doesn't open till six, and we have time to kneel down to say
a few words to our Father first. I think we should all feel
better after that, shouldn't we?"

The red-nosed man was very helpful, pulling the harmo-
nium into place and handing out the prayer-books. His back
was to the lady as he did this, and it was his idea of a joke
to deal the books like a pack of cards, whispering to each
man as he did so, "There y'are, mate."

Bareheaded, we knelt down among the dirty teacups and
began to mumble that we had left undone those things that
we ought to have done, and done those things that we ought
not to have done, and there was no health in us. The
lady prayed very fervently, but her eyes roved over us all
the time, making sure that we were attending. When she was
not looking we grinned and winked at one another, and
whispered bawdy jokes, just to show that we did not care,
but it stuck in our throats a little . . . .

The prayers lasted half an hour, and then after a hand-
shake at the door, we made off. "Well," said somebody as
soon as we were out of hearing, "the trouble's over. I
thought them .... prayers was never goin' to end."

"You had your bun," said another; "you got to pay for it."

"Pray for it, you mean. Ah, you don't get much for
nothing. They can't even give you a twopenny cup of
tea without you going down on your .... knees
for it."[12]

The Church has been slow to learn that God is not honoured
by the reluctant prayers of unhallowed lips, and that the cause
of true religion is not furthered by subsidized hypocrisy.

The Roman Church, Dostoevsky charges, has been guilty of
the most cynical and calculated exploitation. Dostoevsky portrays Jesus returning to seventeenth-century Seville, where the
Spanish Inquisition is busily burning heretics to the greater
glory of God. Jesus raises a little girl of seven years to
life again. He is immediately recognized. The Cardinal sees

[12] *Down and Out in Paris and London* (Berkley, New York, 1959),
pp. 102-3.

everything and orders His arrest. That night the Cardinal visits Him in His cell. He interrogates Jesus, but Jesus remains disturbingly silent. The Cardinal speaks of those temptations which Jesus rejected in the wilderness. He says that "in those three questions the whole subsequent history of mankind is, as it were, brought together in one whole, and foretold, and in them are united all the unresolved contradictions of human nature." Jesus, by refusing to turn stones into loaves of bread, showed man too much respect. "Thou wouldst not deprive man of freedom," he says, "and didst reject the offer, thinking, what is that freedom worth, if obedience is bought with bread? Thou didst reply that man lives not by bread alone. . . . Dost Thou know," he continues, "that the ages will pass, and humanity will proclaim by the lips of their sages that there is no crime, and therefore no sin; there is only hunger?" Food is man's most urgent and imperious need; for food, a man will sacrifice everything that he possesses, even his freedom. "In the end," the Cardinal insists, "they will lay their freedom at our feet, and say to us, 'Make us your slaves, but feed us.'"

In the wilderness, the Cardinal repeats, Jesus was given the opportunity of winning men by turning stones into loaves of bread.

> This is the significance of the first question in the wilderness, and this is what Thou hast rejected for the sake of that freedom which Thou hast exalted above everything. Yet in this question lies the great secret of this world. Choosing 'bread', Thou wouldst have satisfied the universal and everlasting craving of humanity — to find someone to worship. . . . I tell Thee that man is tormented by no greater anxiety than to find someone quickly to whom he can hand over that gift of freedom with which, unhappy creature, he was born. . . . In bread there was offered Thee an invincible banner; give bread, and man will worship Thee, for nothing is more certain than bread. . . . Instead of taking possession of man's freedom, Thou didst increase it, and burdened the spiritual kingdom of mankind with its suffering forever. Thou didst desire man's free love, that he should follow Thee freely, enticed and taken captive by Thee."

Jesus vehemently refused to win men by turning stones into bread. He knew, only too well, that a man cannot live without

bread, but He also knew that a man cannot live by bread alone.
Thomas Carlyle observes that "not all the Finance Ministers
and Upholsterers and Confectioners of modern Europe in joint
stock company" can make "one shoeblack happy . . . above
an hour or two,"[13] and the explanation is that a man's life does
not consist in the abundance of those things which he possesses.
There are, within us all, "immortal longings," which can never
be finally satisfied by the things of this world.   Jesus, in re-
jecting the temptation of the Evil One, recognised this fact:

> Man shall not live by bread alone,
> but by every word that proceeds
> from the mouth of God.

The rejection of the temptation to win men by the exploitation of their physical and material needs was quickly followed in the Gospel narrative by another temptation.

> Then the devil took him to the holy city, and set him on the
> pinnacle of the temple, and said to him, "If you are the
> Son of God, throw yourself down; for it is written, 'He will
> give his angels charge of you, and on their hands they will
> bear you up, lest you strike your foot against a stone.' "
> Jesus said to him, "Again it is written, 'You shall not tempt
> the Lord your God' " (Matthew 4:5-7).

It was easy for the devil to argue that such a prodigious
miracle as that of jumping unharmed and unhurt from the top
of the pinnacle would enable Jesus to provide striking con-
firmation of His divine Sonship and browbeat the people into
belief.   There were many who expected the Messiah to come
from heaven.   What more appropriate way of fulfilling this
expectation than by descending from a pinnacle of the temple
in the full light of day when the courts of the temple were full
of people?   In this way He would, the devil argued, silence His
critics and persuade the crowd.
    The devil was quick to invoke the convenient support of
Scripture by quoting a passage with Messianic associations.
There is graphic beauty in the quotation from the ninety-first
Psalm with its suggestion of angelic protection and carefulness:
"On their hands they will bear you up, lest you strike your foot

---

[13] *Sartor Resartus,* Book 2, Chapter IX.

against a stone." The reply of Jesus was to point out that to court needless danger and to put God to the test is not to trust Him.

The Jews were insistent in their demand for validating signs and wonders. Paul, speaking of his own countrymen, testifies: "Jews demand signs." To Jesus they bluntly said: "Teacher, we wish to see a sign from you" (Matthew 12:38). As He hung on the cross they blasphemously shouted: "Let him come down now from the cross, and we will believe in him" (Matthew 27:42).

Jesus knew that men are not brought to repentance by portents and prodigies. It was Dives, in the torments of Hades, who cried: "If some one goes to them from the dead, they will repent." Jesus knew better: "If they do not hear Moses and the prophets, neither will they be convinced if some one should rise from the dead" (Luke 16:31).

Jesus refused to work miracles for the purpose of compelling belief. "The works that he did," James Denney observes, "were not venturesome audacities of His own; they were the works that the Father gave Him to do."[14] They were not reckless acts of spectacular power but acts of loving service evoked by human need.

Dostoevsky's Inquisitor says that there are three powers, three powers alone, able to conquer and to hold captive forever the consciences of men; those forces, he says, are miracle, mystery, and authority. The Inquisitor continues to admonish Jesus in vain self-extenuation.

> Thou hast rejected all three and hast set the example for doing so. When the wise and dread spirit set Thee on the pinnacle of the temple and said to Thee, 'If Thou wouldst know whether Thou art the Son of God then cast Thyself down, for it is written: the angels shall hold Thee up lest Thou fall and bruise Thyself, and Thou shalt know then whether Thou art the Son of God and shalt prove then how great is Thy faith in Thy Father.' But Thou didst refuse and wouldst not cast Thyself down. Oh!, of course, Thou didst proudly and well, like God; but the weak, unruly race of men, are they gods? . . . Thou didst know that Thy deed would be recorded in books, would be handed down to remote times

14 *The Way Everlasting* (Hodder & Stoughton, London, 1911), p. 196.

and the uttermost ends of the earth, and Thou didst hope
that man, following Thee, would cling to God and not ask
for a miracle. . . .

But as man cannot bear to be without the miraculous, he
will create new miracles of his own for himself, and will
worship deeds of sorcery and witchcraft, though he might be
a hundred times over a rebel, heretic and infidel. Thou didst
not come down from the Cross when they shouted to Thee,
mocking and reviling Thee, 'Come down from the cross and
we will believe that Thou art He!' Thou didst not come down,
for again Thou wouldst not enslave man by a miracle, and
didst crave for free love and not the base raptures of the
slave before the might that has overawed him forever. . . .

The Cardinal Inquisitor speaks of the triumphs which the
Church has been able to accomplish by accepting the temptation which Jesus rejected. "We have corrected Thy work,"
he boldly claims, "and have founded it upon miracle, mystery,
and authority. And men rejoiced that they were again led like
sheep, and that the terrible gift that had brought them such
suffering was, at last, lifted from their hearts. Were we not
right," he insistently demands, "teaching them this? Speak!
Did we not love mankind, so meekly acknowledging their problems, lovingly lightening their burden, and permitting their
weak nature even sin with our sanction?"

The Roman Church, in Dostoevsky's judgment, has capitulated to the temptation which Jesus rejected and has en-
throned, at the centre of its worship, miracle, mystery, and
authority.

Other representatives of organized religion have employed the
techniques of psychological manipulation to engineer and accomplish the conversion of men. In this twentieth century
we have seen how the minds of men — through the sinister
techniques of brain-washing — can be changed. By psychological manipulation and the systematic deprivation of sleep, by
the exploitation of guilt and the inculcation of fear, by intimi-
dation and torture, by induced terror, the minds of men can
be assaulted and assailed until their wills are broken and
brave men are reduced to the whimpering helplessness of little
children. In this state, cowed and broken, unable to resist,
they are puppets in the hands of those who would remake

them in their own image. These ruthless manipulators of the human personality know that sooner or later, given the requisite pressures — both physical and psychological — a man must break. In this state of induced terror, of abject fear, a man is ready to receive any suggestion and to do any deed.

But it is not only the ruthless agents of totalitarian tyranny who have resorted to methods so diabolically destructive of human personality; on occasions, the misguided servants of Jesus Christ have done so, too. This is the substance of William Sargant's disturbing indictment of the Christian Church in his book *Battle for the Mind*. His interest in this matter was first aroused when he read the *Journals* of John Wesley in the library of his father's parsonage. He was struck by the fact that Wesley's authoritarian preaching of imminent damnation was often accompanied by dramatic physical consequences of a distressing kind: tears and shaking tremors and speechlessness and insensibility. Sargent came to the conclusion that Wesley was using, albeit unconsciously, the very methods of psychological battery and physical terror which are used by those who organize, for their Marxist masters, indoctrination courses today.

When the Church is tempted to use miracle, mystery, and authority as a device for winning men and effecting their salvation, we must say what Jesus said when He was tempted to throw Himself from the temple to provoke the saving intervention of God: "You shall not tempt the Lord your God."

> Again, the devil took him to a very high mountain, and showed him all the kingdoms of the world and the glory of them; and he said to him, "All these I will give you, if you will fall down and worship me" (Matthew 4:8-9).

In this third and last temptation Jesus was tempted to win the kingdoms of the world by entering into an easy alliance with evil. Jesus indignantly rejected the suggestion: "Begone, Satan!"

The same temptation to forsake the narrow path of costly obedience for the broader way of convenient accommodation was renewed by the chief of His apostles at Caesarea Philippi. In a blinding flash of sudden illumination, Peter glimpsed the truth — that Jesus was none other than the promised Messiah.

In response to the question of Jesus: "But who do you say that I am?" Peter replied: "You are the Christ, the Son of the living God." Jesus was deeply moved: and then He began to explain to them what Messiahship meant: it meant obedience to a lonely vocation of rejection and suffering and death. Peter was stunned by this scandalous talk of suffering and death. He immediately expostulated: "God forbid, Lord! This shall never happen to you." Jesus turned on Peter with words of terrifying condemnation: "Get behind me, Satan! You are a hindrance to me; for you are not on the side of God, but of men" (Matthew 16:13-23).

Jesus recognised in Peter's well-meaning but misguided words a renewal of the third temptation. Jesus recognised the proposal as nothing less than a diabolic attempt to frustrate and defeat the declared purposes of God.

Again and again the Church has been tempted to accept the temptation which Jesus so indignantly rejected, and has been persuaded to adopt the easy way of moral compromise and vacillating accommodation.

Dostoevsky insists that the Roman Church has also succumbed to this third and last temptation. He portrays the Grand Inquisitor, in the presence of the silent and disturbing Christ, defiantly seeking to justify the Church's cynical betrayal of its Lord. The Cardinal freely admits that the Church has taken the side of the devil:

> We are not working with Thee, but with *him* — that is our mystery. It's long — eight centuries — since we have been on *his* side and not on Thine. Just eight centuries ago, we took from him what Thou didst reject with scorn, that last gift he offered Thee, showing Thee all the kingdoms of the earth. We took from him Rome and the sword of Caesar, and proclaimed ourselves sole rulers of the earth. . . . Thou mightest have taken even then the sword of Caesar. Why didst Thou reject that last gift? Hadst Thou accepted that last counsel of the mighty spirit, Thou wouldst have accomplished all that man seeks on earth — that is, someone to worship, someone to keep his conscience, and some means of uniting all in one unanimous and harmonious antheap, for the craving for universal unity is the third and last anguish of men. . . . We have taken the sword of Caesar, and in taking it, of course, have rejected Thee and followed

him. . . . With us all will be happy and will no more rebel nor destroy one another as under Thy freedom. . . . We shall show them that they are weak, that they are only pitiful children, but that childlike happiness is the sweetest of all. They will become timid and will look to us and huddle close to us in fear. . . . They will marvel at us and will be awe-stricken before us, and will be proud at our being so power-ful and clever. Oh, we shall allow them even sin, they are weak and helpless, and they will love us like children because we allow them to sin. We shall tell them that every sin will be expiated, if it is done with our permission, that we allow them to sin because we love them, and the punishment for their sins we take upon ourselves. And we shall take it upon ourselves, and they will adore us as their saviours who have taken on their sins before God. And they will have no secrets from us. We shall allow or forbid them to live with their wives and mistresses, to have or not to have children — according to whether they have been obedient or disobedient — and they will submit to us gladly and cheerfully. The most painful secrets of their conscience, all, all they will bring to us, and we shall have an answer for all. All will be happy. . . .

Dostoevsky catalogues with painful particularity the methods by which the Roman Church, in its pursuit of sovereignty and power, has sought to win the allegiance of men by unscrupu-lously sanctioning superstition and casuistically condoning sin. But that is not all. The Roman Church, Dostoevsky insists, has made crime a virtue.

It is not difficult to multiply examples. After the treacherous Massacre of St. Bartholomew's Day (August 23, 1572), the bells of St. Peter's, Rome, were pealed in joy, medals were struck, and a Solemn *Te Deum* of Thanksgiving was sung. Pope Gregory VIII summoned the eminent painter Vasari from Florence to celebrate the triumph of the massacre in a series of frescoes.

But Protestants are not without sin. When Luther condoned the secret bigamy of Philip of Hesse he was guilty of subordinat-ing principle to expediency and morality to politics. Philip of Hesse had given yeoman service to the cause of the Protestant Reformation. He was a statesman of unusual ability. He had, however, developed a profound physical aversion for his wife. It was in these circumstances that Luther agreed that he might, with a good conscience, take to himself a second wife, provided that the relationship was not made public. When the scandal broke Luther counselled a lie. His advice had been given, he said, in the confessional, and under Canon Law a priest is permitted to tell a lie to guard the secrets of the confessional. It is a sordid and discreditable episode in the history of the Reformation. The plain fact is that Luther, at Philip's urgent insistence, allowed himself to jettison the plain obligations of morality. He thereby gave his suffrage to the Evil One. He capitulated to the third temptation.

It is dangerously easy to justify, on the specious ground of expediency, the commission of that which is evil. Down the ages the Church, since the time of Constantine, has acted on the assumption that the battles of God can be fought with the weapons of the devil and that the faith *can* be extended by the power of the sword. In 1887 the encyclical *Defensa Catolica* declared that "true charity consists in opposing one's neighbour, in injuring him in his material interests, in insulting him and in taking his life, always supposing that it is done for the love of God." Lord Acton, in a review of the events of the past, says that the Church has been guilty of abrogating the plain precepts of morality, and that men, in the service of religion, have become demons. "The papacy," he grimly observes, "made the principle of assassination a law of the Christian Church and a condition of salvation."[15]

Of course, in every age there have been a few splendid souls who have refused to embrace these sanguinary doctrines. Bernard of Clairvaux may be taken as an example. We must win men, he says, not by arms, but by arguments. Roger Williams, echoing Castellio,[16] asks: "Can the sword of steel or arm of flesh make men faithful or loyal to God?"[17] Samuel Butler points out that

> He that complies against his will,
> Is of his own opinion still.

[15] *Selections from the Correspondence of the First Lord Acton* (London, 1917), p. 55.
[16] *Concerning Heretics: whether they are to be persecuted.*
[17] *The Bloody Tenent Yet More Bloody* (1644).

Milton, in *Paradise Regained,* depicts the Saviour declining
to establish His kingdom by constraint, holding it rather "more
humane, more heavenly, first by winning words to conquer
willing hearts and make persuasion do the work of fear."[18]
"Faith," says Luther finely, "is a free work to which no one
can be forced. It is a divine work of the Spirit. Let alone
then that outward force should compel or create it."[19] Un-
fortunately, Luther did not always abide by his own best in-
sights. In relation to the followers of the "Roman Sodom"
he demands: "Why do we not assault them with all arms and
wash our hands in their blood?" But Luther ought to be
judged by his better moments rather than his worse:

> What mad folk we have so long been, who have wished to
> force the Turk to the faith with the sword, the heretic with
> fire, and the Jews with death, to root out the tares with our
> own power, as if we were the people who could rule over
> hearts and spirits and make them religious and good, which
> God's Word must do.[20]

Today it is generally recognised that the use of coercion is
incompatible with the example of our Lord Jesus Christ.
Calvin's successors and loyal sons have set an example by
erecting in Geneva a monument of expiation for the burning
of Servetus. Confronted by the invincible obstinacy of men, it
is tempting for believers to say what the disciples said to Jesus,
after the Samaritan village had refused to receive them, "Lord,
do you want us to bid fire come down from heaven and consume
them?" But such a question is asked in tragic forgetfulness
of the fact that the Son of Man came into the world not to
destroy men's lives but to save them.

Jesus rejected the third temptation of the Evil One — to
win the kingdoms of the world by a sinful accommodation with
evil. Jesus knew that God's work must be done in God's way.
He would win men by nothing save the cross, and He would
offer to men nothing but a cross. He would neither bribe nor
compel.

[18] *Paradise Regained,* lines, 222-3.
[19] Quoted, R. H. Bainton, *The Reformation of the Sixteenth Century*
(Hodder & Stoughton, London, 1953), p. 225.
[20] Quoted Cecil Northcott, *Religious Liberty* (S. C. M., London,
1948), p. 27.

The faithful follower of Christ is under a like limitation in relation to means. "If any man would come after me," Jesus says, "let him deny himself and take up his cross and follow me. . . . For what will it profit a man, if he gains the whole world and forfeits his life?" (Matthew 16:24-26). It is a malicious slander, according to the Apostle Paul, to say that we are willing to do evil that good may come, and those who make this accusation, the Apostle adds indignantly, deserve damnation (Romans 3:8). The Christian man knows that, in the service of Incarnate Love, he is to do that which is honest in the sight of all men, not being overcome by evil but overcoming evil with good.

Brother Ass

or

the mystery of love

Love is strong as death. . . .
Its flashes are flashes of fire,
a most vehement flame (Song of Solomon, 8:6).

Historically, C. S. Lewis says, men have tended to adopt one of three different views in relation to the body.

> First there is that of those ascetic Pagans who called it the prison or the "tomb" of the soul, and of Christians like Fisher to whom it was a "sack of dung", food for worms, filthy, shameful, a source of nothing but temptation to bad men and humiliation to good ones. Then there are the Neo-Pagans (they seldom know Greek), the nudists and the sufferers from Dark Gods, to whom the body is glorious. But thirdly we have the view which St. Francis expressed by calling his body "Brother Ass".[1]

Natural man has tended to alternate uneasily between the opposite extremes of contemptuous denigration and extravagant deification, whereas what is required, on the part of the Christian man, is joyous and humble acceptance. The Apostle Paul exhorts Christians to use the world without abusing it

---

[1] *The Four Loves* (Geoffrey Bles, London, 1960), p. 116.

(1 Corinthians 7:31, A.V.), and his words apply equally
well to the body. It is to be used and not abused; it is neither
to be recklessly mutilated on the one hand, nor weakly indulged on the other; it is to be held in honor, treated with
respect, and disciplined for the service of God. "Now the
stick and now the carrot," says C. S. Lewis succinctly. Commenting more largely on St. Francis' suggestive metaphor,
"Brother Ass," he says: "Ass is exquisitely right because
no-one in his senses can either revere or hate a donkey. It
is a useful, sturdy, lazy, obstinate, patient, lovable and in-
furiating beast; deserving now the stick and now the carrot;
both pathetically and absurdly beautiful. So the body."[2] "The
fact that we have bodies," says C. S. Lewis, "is the oldest joke
there is." There is, particularly in the body's expression of
Eros, he affirms, "an element not only of comedy, not only
of play, but even of buffoonery," which adds to the total
experience "its own grotesque charm."[3] The sublime and the
ridiculous are to be found together, he believes, in the act
of physical intercourse. "The highest does not stand without
the lowest. There is indeed at certain moments a high poetry

---

[2] One is reminded of G. K. Chesterton's moving little poem:

> *When fishes flew and forests walked*
> *And figs grew upon thorn,*
> *Some moment when the moon was blood*
> *Then surely I was born;*
>
> *With monstrous head and sickening cry*
> *And ears like errant wings,*
> *The devil's walking parody*
> *Of all four-footed things.*
>
> *The tattered outlaw of the earth,*
> *Of ancient crooked will;*
> *Starve, scourge, deride me: I am dumb,*
> *I keep my secret still.*
>
> *Fools! For I also had my hour;*
> *One far fierce hour and sweet:*
> *There was a shout about my ears,*
> *And palms before my feet.*

[3] C. S. Lewis, *op. cit.,* p. 117.

in the flesh itself; but also, by your leave, an irreducible element of obstinate and ludicrous un-poetry."

It is the disconcerting presence of poetry and un-poetry, of gravity and levity, of the sublime and the grotesque, that puzzles and perplexes the reflective man.

"There is something mysterious or uncanny about the beginning and end of life," Dean Inge avers, "which Nature has associated with circumstances in the one case offensive to modesty, and in the other horrible."[4]   C. S. Lewis quotes Sir Thomas Browne's embarrassed apology for the act of intercourse: it is, he says, "the foolishest act a wise man commits in all his life, nor is there anything that will more deject his cooled imagination, when he shall consider what an odd and unworthy piece of folly he had committed."

It is not surprising that there are those who have been tempted to contemptuous denigration.   They are embarrassed by the fact that we have bodies (Porphyry, according to his contemporaries, seemed ashamed of his body and thanked God that he had not been made with an immortal body), and that we reproduce ourselves in the way that we do.   It is all, they feel, faintly discreditable if not disgusting.

Literature, as well as religion, has its Manichaeans, according to Aldous Huxley, "men who on principle would exile the body and its functions from the world of their art, who condemn as vulgar all too particular and detailed accounts of physical actuality, as vulgar any attempt to relate mental or spiritual events to happenings in the body."   These writers create characters, Huxley bluntly asserts, who "are not human beings, but tragical heroes and heroines who never blow their noses."[5]

G. K. Chesterton, speaking of Bernard Shaw, says: "All there is of him is excellent only he happens to be wholly lacking in certain parts of human nature which, to the majority of us, are fundamental."   William Temple points out that Shaw can discuss the problem of "getting married" in a charming *Conversation in Three Acts* without alluding to anything like

[4] *The End of an Age* (Putman, London, 1948), p. 71.

[5] "Vulgarity in Literature," *Collected Essays* (Chatto & Windus, London, 1960), p. 107.

human passion. The characters discuss the problem so charm-
ingly, he adds, "that one forgets that it has no relation to
anything whatever that happens in human life." The absence
of human passion is due to a fundamental aversion to what
he regards as the cloying contamination of the body. In
Back to Methusaleh it is significant that "the Ancients" look
forward to discarding their bodies as Shaw believes they once
discarded their tails.[6] In *Man and Superman* the same point
is made with unambiguous particularity: "This earth is a nursery in which men and women play at being heroes and heroines,
saints and sinners, but they are dragged down from their
fool's paradise by their bodies." In the life to come, however,
"you escape this tyranny of the flesh . . . you are not an animal
at all; you are a ghost, an appearance, an illusion, a convention,
deathless, ageless, in a word bodiless."[7]

Shaw, in this matter, does not stand alone. T. E. Lawrence's
aversion to all things physical was almost pathological. "To
put my hand on a living thing was defilement," he tells us in
The Seven Pillars of Wisdom, "and it made me tremble if they
touched me or took too great an interest in me. There was an
atomic repulsion."[8] His brutal humiliation at the hands of
the Turks in Deraa remained a bitter, obsessive memory. He
felt that the citadel of his integrity had been irrevocably lost.[9]
He had always been nervously inhibited, but now, more than
ever, he became morbidly terrified of physical contact. "I had
a longing for the absolutism of women and animals," he confesses unhappily, "and lamented myself most when I saw a
soldier with a girl or a man fondling a dog, because my wish
was to be as superficial, as perfected; and my jailor held me

---

[6] G. K. Chesterton maintains that Shaw's evolutionism is rooted in
a fundamental "desperation about man" and he contrasts Shaw's belief
with the Christian doctrine of the resurrection, "of the *whole* of man."
"We do not believe," he says, "that man is a mass of mistakes that
have to be shed until he has lost everything but shame and the very
memory of his manhood." *George Bernard Shaw* (Guild Books, London, 1951), pp. 124-6.

[7] *Man and Superman,* Act III.

[8] *The Seven Pillars of Wisdom* (Jonathan Cape, London, 1946),
p. 580.

[9] *Ibid.,* p. 456.

back."[10] He resented the fact that his friends talked freely
"of food and illness, games and pleasures." He felt that
"to recognize our possession of bodies was degradation
enough without enlarging upon their failings and attributes."
"I would feel shame for myself," he tells us, "at seeing them
wallow in the physical which could be only a glorification of
man's cross."[11]

It is not surprising that he regarded his own physical self
with profound distaste. Stephen Neill draws attention to those
cruel little sketches, so characteristic of *The Seven Pillars,* in
which Lawrence appears to take a masochistic pleasure in
holding up to ridicule the humiliating absurdity and weakness
of his body.[12]

There are many who turn from sex with loathing, aversion,
and disgust, and who, as a consequence, despise the body.
This is the heresy of Manichaeism. And the danger of Manichaeism is always emasculation, whether in literature or in
life. In Shakespeare, William Temple says, we have "the real
passions of human nature," whereas what we have in many
modern playwrights, by contrast, is "mere surface and veneer,
overlaying the volcanic forces of life which are genuinely
within us, which we conceal because we are so much afraid of
them."[13] Aldous Huxley gives a further illustration. He describes French classical tragedies as "the most completely
Manichaean works of art ever created." He says that in them

> lust itself has ceased to be corporeal and takes its place
> among the other abstract symbols, with which the authors
> write their strange algebraical equations of passion and con-
> flict. . . . Manichaeans, the classical writers confined them-
> selves exclusively to the study of man as a creature of pure
> reason and discarnate passions . . . By the very act of im-
> posing limitations the classicists were enabled to achieve a
> certain universality of statement impossible to those who
> attempt to reproduce the particularities and incompletenesses

[10] *Ibid.,* p. 581.

[11] *Ibid.,* p. 584.

[12] *Foundation Beliefs* (The Christian Literature Society for India,
Madras, 1941), p. 46.

[13] A. E. Baker, ed., *William Temple's Teaching* (James Clarke, London, n.d.), p. 175.

of actual corporeal life. But what they gained in universality, they lost in vivacity and immediate truth. You cannot get something for nothing.[14]

It is tempting for one to react against the denigration of the body by falling into a contrary error, an exaggerated exaltation of the body almost indistinguishable from deification. This is the error of Naturalism.

In the sexual experience D. H. Lawrence discovered not only the intense joys of physical fulfillment but, in some mysterious way, the key to the secret and meaning of life. "My great religion," Lawrence writes, "is a belief in the blood, the flesh, as being wiser than the intellect. We can go wrong with the mind. But what the blood feels, and believes, and says, is always true." Speaking of sex, Lawrence says: "Sex should come upon us as a terrible thing of suffering and privilege and mystery: a mysterious metamorphosis is come upon us, and a new terrible power given us, and a new responsibility. . . . The mystery, the terror and the tremendous power of sex should never be explained away. . . . The mystery must remain in its dark secrecy, and its dark, powerful dynamism." Lawrence was zealously eager to save sex from libertarian profanation and to affirm its sanctity. For Lawrence sex was an absolute — holy, terrible and beautiful. "I always labour at the same thing," he says, "to make the sex relation valid and precious instead of shameful." "To me," he repeats, "it is beautiful and tender as the naked self." He disapproved of casual sex, of sex without love, of promiscuous sex. He insisted that the act of physical intercourse between a man and a woman, as an expression and consequence of their love, is always something healthy, desirable, and good.

Lawrence was a doughty crusader on behalf of romantic love, whom he stoutly declares to be no wanton. Nevertheless, as her devotees find, she is an imperious lady, and she brooks no opposition, least of all the petty restraints of such institutional conventions as marriage. For Lawrence, the demands of love are supreme and brook no denial. What we need to do, he repeats, is to recognize the primacy of love and its legitimate expression in the act of unashamed sexual inter-

---

[14] A. Huxley, *op. cit.,* p. 108.

course.   In *A propos of Lady Chatterley's Lover,* Lawrence
writes:

> We are today, as human beings, evolved and cultured far
> beyond the taboos which are inherent in our culture. . . .
> In the past, man was too weak-minded, or crude-minded, to
> contemplate his own physical functions, without getting all
> messed up with physical reactions that overpowered him.
> It is no longer so. . . . I want men and women to be able
> to think sex, fully, completely, honestly and clearly. . . .
> Years of honest thought of sex, and years of struggling action
> in sex will bring us at last where we want to get, to our real
> and accomplished chastity, our completeness, when our sex-
> ual act and our sexual thought are in harmony, and the one
> does not interfere with the other.[15]

Lawrence emphatically denies that he is sanctioning or condoning sexual licence.   "Far be it from me to suggest that all
women should go running after game keepers for lovers. Far
be it from me to suggest that they should be running after
anybody.   A great many men and women are happiest when
they abstain and stay sexually apart, quite clean:[16] and, at the
same time, when they understand and realize sex more fully."
Lawrence's concern is to rescue sex from desecration and de-
humanization and to affirm its binding character and essential
sacredness.   He freely acknowledges the contribution which
Christianity has made to an exalted understanding of marriage
and of the place of sex in it.

> Christianity brought marriage into the world: marriage as
> we know it.   Christianity established the little autonomy of
> the family within the greater rule of the State.   Christianity
> made marriage in some respects inviolate, not to be violated
> by the State.   It is marriage, perhaps, which has given man
> the best of his freedom, given him his little kingdom of his

---

[15] Quoted, *The Trial of Lady Chatterley,* Regina v. Penguin Books
Ltd. (edited by C. H. Rolph). (Penguin Books, Harmondsworth, Middx.,
1961), p. 79.

[16] Lawrence's use of the word "clean" to describe sexual abstinence
is extraordinarily revealing.   Does he, in spite of protestations, imply
that there is something "unclean" about sexual intercourse? Does this reveal an unsuspected strain of Manichaeanism?   See my article, "Literature has its Manichaeans," *The Reformed Theological Review,* Vol.
XXII, No. 1. (February, 1963).

own within the big Kingdom of the State, given him his foot-
hold of independence on which to stand and resist an unjust
State.   Man and wife, a king and queen with one or two sub-
jects and a few square yards of territory of their own: this,
really, is marriage.   It is a true freedom because it is a true ful-
filment, for man, woman, and children. . . .   And the Church
created marriage by making it a sacrament, a sacrament of
man and woman united in the sex communion, and never to
be separated, except by death.   And even when separated
by death, still not freed from the marriage.   Marriage, as far
as the individual went, eternal.   Marriage, making one complete body out of two incomplete ones, and providing for the
complex development of the man's soul and the woman's
soul in union, under the spiritual rule of the Church.[17]

Lawrence adds: "I realize that marriage, or something like it,
is essential, and that the old church knew best the enduring
needs of man, beyond the spasmodic needs of today and
yesterday."   Then, having said all this, Lawrence interjects
a characteristic qualification: "But — and this 'but' crashes
through our hearts like a bullet — marriage is no marriage that
is not basically and permanently phallic, and that is not linked
up with the sun and the earth, the moon and the fixed stars
and the planets, in the rhythm of days, in the rhythm of months,
in the rhythm of quarters, of years, of decades, and of centuries."

It is not surprising that Lawrence interprets the sexual experience in religious terms and that he associates with it such
religious experiences as moral cleansing and ritual purity.   It
is Lady Chatterley reflecting:

She had to be a passive consenting thing, like a slave, a
physical slave.   Yet the passion licked round her, consum-
ing, and when the sensual flame of it pressed through her
bowels and breast, she really thought she was dying: yet a
poignant death.   She had often wondered what Abelard
meant, when he said that in their year of love he and Heloise
had passed through all the stages and refinements of passion.
The same thing a thousand years ago!   The same on the
Greek vases, everywhere!   The refinements of passion, the
extravagance of sensuality!   And necessary, forever neces-

17 Quoted, *The Trial of Lady Chatterley,* p. 160.

sary, to burn out false shames and smelt out the heaviest ore
of the body into purity. With the fire of sheer sensuality.
In the short summer night she learnt so much. She would
have thought a woman would have died of shame. Instead
of which the shame died. Shame, which is fear; the deep
organic shame, the old, old physical fear which crouches in
the bodily roots of us, and can only be chased away by the
sensual fire, at last it was roused up and routed by the
phallic hunt of the man. . . .[18]

It is, of course, a short step from the glorification of sexuality to its "deification." There is, says the preacher of Eccle-
siastes, nothing new under the sun. Centuries ago, in Asia
Minor, the fertility cults had their phallic worship in which
the processes of reproduction and the act of intercourse were
celebrated and adored. In like manner, there are those today
who find the significance of life in erotic excitation and unre-
strained sensual enjoyment. Walt Whitman praises sex as the
compendium of all meaning and the quintessence of reality.

Sex contains all, bodies, souls,
Meanings, proofs, purities, delicacies, results,
    promulgations,
Songs, commands, health, pride, the maternal mystery,
    the seminal milk,
All hopes, benefactions, bestowals, all the passions,
    loves, beauties, delights of the earth,
All the governments, judges, gods, follow'd persons
    of the earth,
These are contain'd in sex as parts of itself and
    justifications of itself.[19]

Whitman's panegyric might even leave Freud a little breathless.
There is something ironic in the fact that it is the poet Whitman,
whose own sex life was notoriously disordered and perverse,
who sings the praise of the sexual experience as the supreme
revelation of life.

Idolatry is the consequence of deification and idolatry always
leads to humiliating bondage and moral corruption. They

[18] *Ibid.,* p. 222.
[19] "A woman waits for me," *Walt Whitman,* Complete Poetry and
Selected Prose and Letters, Emory Holloway, ed. (Nonesuch Press, London, 1938), p. 96.

that make to themselves idols, the Psalmist bluntly says, are like unto them (Psalm 135:18, A.V.). There is, says the Apostle Paul, an inseparable connection between idolatry and immorality (Romans 1).

Norman Mailer describes the post-war Beat generation for whom the significance of the sexual experience is no longer the self-surrender of love but the act of physical orgasm. Today, he says, we regard love not "as the search for a mate, but love as the search for an orgasm more apocalyptic than the one which preceded it." Thus, for the "hipster," God "is located in the senses of the body"; "not," he hastens to add, "the God of the churches but the unachievable whisper of mystery within the sex, the paradise of limitless energy and perception just beyond the next wave of the next orgasm."[20]

Aldous Huxley, in his bitter satire *Ape and Essence,* portrays the deformed monstrosities who have survived the nuclear destruction of World War III, among whom love has degenerated into lust and sadism, and whose sole interest is the frantic and feverish pursuit of multiplied orgasm. Huxley describes a typical scene which takes place in the concert hall. A female baboon, "in shell pink evening gown, her mouth painted purple, her muzzle painted mauve, her fiery red eyes ringed with mascara," appears on the stage dragging behind her, "on all fours and secured by a light steel chain attached to a dog collar," Michael Faraday. She is about to sing when she catches sight of Faraday on his knees, in the act of straightening his bent and aching back. "Down, sir, down!" The tone is peremptory; she gives the old man a cut with her switch. Faraday winces and obeys; the audience laughs delightedly. She blows them a kiss, and then she sings the latest popular success:

> *Love, Love, Love —*
> *Love's the very essence*
> *Of everything I think, of everything I do.*
> *Give me, Give me, Give me,*
> *Give me detumescence*
> *That means you.*

[20] *The Beat Generation and the Angry Young Men,* Gene Feldman and Max Gartenberg, eds. (Dell, New York, 1959), pp. 382, 389.

Thus, what begins as the deification of sex ends in the awful degradation of crude animality.

D. H. Lawrence recognized the danger. He resented the fact that there are those who are ready to degrade sex and to prostitute it in the service of perversity and lust. It made him angry and disgusted. Mellors, Lawrence's mouthpiece in *Lady Chatterley's Lover,* comments bitterly: "I feel the Colonies aren't far enough. The moon wouldn't be far enough, because you could look back and see the earth, dirty, beastly, unsavoury, among the stars; made foul by men." In *Sons and Lovers* Lawrence relates an incident which is clearly a traumatic childhood memory:

> Often Paul would wake up, after he had been asleep a long while, aware of thuds downstairs. Instantly he was wide awake. Then he heard the booming shouts of his father, come home nearly drunk, then the sharp replies of his mother, then the bang, bang, of his father's fist on the table, and the nasty snarling shout as the man's voice got higher. And then the whole was drowned in a piercing medley of shrieks and cries from the great wind-swept ash tree. The children lay silent in suspense, waiting for a lull in the wind to hear what their father was doing. He might hit their mother again. There was a feeling of horror, a kind of bristling in the darkness, and a sense of blood. They lay with their hearts in the grip of an intense anguish. The wind came through the tree fiercer and fiercer. All the chords of the great harp hummed, whistled and shrieked.

D. H. Lawrence never erased from his sensitive imagination those early memories of fierce animal passion and sexual outrage, "the imbecile earnestness of lust."

There is a third possibility in relation to the body and the fact of human sexuality: neither denigration, nor deification, but glad and humble and frank acceptance. It finds expression in an attitude of delighted joy and high privilege. It believes that God has given us all things richly to enjoy (1 Timothy 6:17), and that enjoyment is not compatible with an inhibiting sense of morbid guilt and anxious concern. Sex is a high and holy privilege; what is required for its full and satisfying enjoyment is humble thankfulness and joyous self-surrender.

We have tended, by our anxious preoccupation with techniques and a familiarity with diagrammatic detail, to make the subject of sex dull. We have banished gaiety and spontaneity; we have, in our earnest and unimaginative way, desecrated the mystery by thinking coldly of hygienic necessity. C. S. Lewis observes: "The moderns have achieved the feat, which I should have thought impossible, of making the whole subject a bore. Poor Aphrodite! They have sandpapered most of the Homeric laughter off her face." Sex, rightly understood, is ecstasy and great joy. Because it is a gift it is also a trust; it is neither to be prostituted nor profaned. Whatever you do, says the Apostle, do all to the glory of God (1 Corinthians 10:31).

For the Christian man there is nothing evil about the body. Luther draws attention to the fact that our Lord, who was *sinless,* had a body, and that the devil, who is *sinful,* is without a body. The body, as such, is not sinful, although it can be used in the service of sin. It is not (as the Greeks thought) a tomb; on the contrary, it is rather (as the Apostle Paul taught) a temple (1 Corinthians 6:19). It is not disgusting; it is not degrading. On the contrary, it is a thing of holiness and excellent beauty.

The body is not an embarrassing encumbrance to the soul; on the contrary, it is a necessary vehicle for the expression of personality. That is why Christians do not think of immortality in the life to come, but of resurrection. They do not look forward to a disembodied existence, but to a life in which all is transfigured and transformed. In that new life the body will no longer be subject to sin and sickness, but will be resplendent and altogether glorious.

We are, says the Psalmist, "fearfully and wonderfully made" (Psalm 139:14, A.V.). That is why we ought to be humble and grateful; that is why we ought to treat the body with honour and respect. It is the handiwork of God; it is God's good gift. "Everything created by God is good," according to the Apostle, "and nothing is to be rejected if it is received with thanksgiving; for then it is consecrated by the word of God and prayer" (1 Timothy 4:4). Thus, the body is not "nasty," but good; it is not unclean, but holy; it is not to be rejected, but received with thanksgiving.

The Christian fathers had such a high view of the body and reverent respect for the fact of sexuality that some of them held that, before the Fall, the pleasures of intercourse were infinitely greater than they are now. Albertus Magnus believed that in his state of innocence, man, knowing perfect sensitivity, enjoyed the most exquisite joys of pure love.

It has become a convention to insist that the Bible knows nothing of romantic love: romantic love, we are told, was a late discovery of the troubadours of Provence. But Jacob, the Bible says, worked seven years for Rachel, "and they seemed to him but a few days because of the love he had for her" (Genesis 29:20). Every lover knows this experience. Here at any rate, the reality of romantic love is recognized and affirmed. Of course, more primitive views of marriage as a matter of negotiation and arrangement are also to be found. Nevertheless, in the Bible we find an early recognition of the fact that marriage is pleasurable and beautiful as well as useful and necessary.

The fullest expression of this is to be found in the *Song of Solomon,* which probably contains the most moving and sublime erotic poetry in all literature. It describes a love which is as passionate and as "hungry as the sea." The climax of the poem is in the tremendous and triumphant declaration that "love is as strong as death." According to the testimony of Milton *(On Education),* true poetry is "simple, sensuous and passionate," and, judged by these criteria, the Song of Solomon is true poetry of a superlative order.

The lovers are aware of the inexhaustible ramifications of love and the exquisite delights of a pure sensuality. "O that you would kiss me with the kisses of your mouth!" "O that his left hand were under my head, and that his right hand embraced me!" She waits impatiently for his arrival, and then she hears the lift of the latch: "My beloved put his hand to the latch and my heart was thrilled within me."

The lovers find endless delight in each other. The swain speaks exultantly of the beauty of her eyes and lips and mouth: "Your eyes are doves behind your veil." "Your lips are like a scarlet thread and your mouth is lovely." "You are all fair, my love; there is no flaw in you." His heart melts within him: "You have ravished my heart, my sister, my bride, you have ravished my heart with a glance of your eyes." He is conscious of being the unworthy recipient of a love which is precious and beyond compare:

> How sweet is your love, my sister,
>   my bride!
> how much better is your love
>   than wine,
> and the fragrance of your oils
>   than any spice!
> Your lips distil nectar, my bride;
> honey and milk are under your
>   tongue;
> the scent of your garments is like
>   the scent of Lebanon.

She responds to his love with her love. She rejoices in the fact that she is his and he is hers. "I am my beloved's and my beloved is mine." In the dissolving ecstasy of love she cries aloud: "I am sick with love." She rejoices in the assurance of his devotion, in the precious exclusiveness of his love. "I am my beloved's, and his desire is for me." She is eager to give herself in the fullness of physical self-surrender:

> Come, my beloved,
>   let us go forth into the fields,
>   and lodge in the villages;
> let us go out early to the vineyards,
>   and see whether the vines have budded,
> whether the grape blossoms have opened
>   and the pomegranates are in bloom.
> There I will give you my love.

This is the authentic language of voluptuous desire, the pure language of true love.

Hugh Thomson Kerr draws attention to the fact that each lover exhausts the exaggerated language of poetic hyperbole. She uses every rhetorical device of metaphor and simile to describe his beauty:

> My beloved is all radiant and ruddy,
>   distinguished among ten thousand.
> His head is the finest gold;
>   his locks are wavy,
>   black as a raven.

His eyes are like doves
*   beside springs of water,*
bathed in milk,
*   fitly set.*
His cheeks are like beds of spices,
*   yielding fragrance.*
His lips are lilies,
*   distilling liquid myrrh.*
His arms are rounded gold,
*   set with jewels.*
His body is ivory work,
*   encrusted with sapphires.*
His legs are alabaster columns,
*   set upon bases of gold.*
His appearance is like Lebanon,
*   choice as the cedars.*

Finally, words fail; she can only say: "He is altogether desirable."

He also uses the ornate and extravagant language of poetic exaggeration. He praises her eyes and hair and teeth and lips and cheeks and neck and breasts until, again, words fail, and he can only say: "Behold, you are beautiful, my love, behold, you are beautiful!" This agonizing shuttle between verbose description and the realization of the insufficiency of words is, says Hugh Thomson Kerr, part of the poignancy of love.

True love is always jealous and exclusive. It is never promiscuous; on the contrary, it is intensely personal. "I am yours . . . You are mine." Each belongs to the other in a relationship which is as exclusive as it is private. "My beloved is mine and I am his."

The poem concludes with a paean in praise of love:

love is strong as death,
*   jealousy is cruel as the grave,*
Its flashes are flashes of fire,
*   a most vehement flame.*
Many waters cannot quench love,
*   neither can floods drown it.*

Love is invincible and irresistible; it is victorious over every obstacle. It is beyond price: "If a man offered for love all the wealth of his house, it would be utterly scorned."

According to the Song of Solomon sexual love is not a matter for embarrassed apology, but for glad and joyous acceptance. The Bible lends no encouragement to those who would deny the reality of the physical in the interests of an ethereal and emasculated spirituality; on the contrary, the Bible sanctifies the physical by insisting that children are a blessing of the Lord.

Historically, men have tended to oscillate, in relation to the body, between Manichaean denigration and Romantic deification. The Christian man will seek to avoid both extremes: on the one hand, the barrenness of a self-stultifying asceticism and, on the other, the corruption of a degrading sensuality. The Bible sanctions neither forced and frantic repression nor the feverish pursuit of orgasm; on the contrary, the Bible states emphatically: "Let marriage be held in honor among you, and let the marriage bed be undefiled; for God will judge the immoral and adulterous" (Hebrews 13:4).

The Christian man glorifies God when he accepts, humbly and gratefully, the privileges and joys of physical love. But the privileges imply responsibilities, and the privilege of love carries with it, as a necessary concomitant, the obligation of fidelity. "This is the will of God," writes St. Paul, "your sanctification: that you abstain from immorality; that each one of you know how to take a wife for himself in holiness and honor, not in the passion of lust like heathen who do not know God" (1 Thessalonians 4:3-5).

Dean Inge rightly observes that when sex ceases to be a mystery, when it ceases to be held "in sanctification and honour," it becomes poisonous. Then, what is meant for man's highest fulfillment becomes the means of his lowest degradation. *Corruptio optimi pessima*: the best, when it is corrupted, becomes the worst. The ineluctible rule is this: the higher we may rise, the lower we may fall. As every lover knows, the experience of love is a noble and uplifting thing, a transforming experience of joy and great gladness, a transfiguration of heaven and earth. But what was given for man's blessing can also become the instrument of man's damnation; love can be degraded into lust, passion into promiscuity, sensuality into perversity.

All this is true. There is about love an urgency, an insist-

146 THE MARK OF CAIN

ency, an imperiousness, which brooks neither denial nor opposition. "Its flashes are flashes of fire, a most vehement flame." That is why it needs to be disciplined and directed in lifelong dedication to the service of the one to whom one is bound by the tie of love. The ancient legal maxim is *abusus non tollit usum,* abuse does not bar use. On every hand there are incitements to carnal self-indulgence, to exploitative experimentation, to the dangerous seductions of perversity; the Christian man who is wise knows that, for the preservation of the mystery and the sanctity of sex, he needs the sanctifying grace of God. "For this reason," Jesus said, "a man shall leave his father and mother and be joined to his wife, and the two shall become one" (Matthew 19:5). In the intimate meeting of marriage, for the Christian man, the mystery of sexuality is revealed and the two are made one.

Epilogue

John A. Mackay points out that the legendary experiences of Robinson Crusoe, as related by Daniel Defoe, parallel, in a striking manner, the experiences of those intrepid pioneers who first came to the shores of America. "Robinson Crusoe," he writes, "was hurled upon an inhospitable shore from a wrecked ship, borne upon the crests of ocean billows. So came the Pilgrims to 'this American wilderness'. Leaving England in a political tempest, they weathered storms on the western ocean, and settled at last in the least suitable part of the Atlantic seaboard." Robinson Crusoe, he continues, "was obliged to work or perish. He accordingly set himself to labour and transferred his island home into a garden. So worked the Puritans in arid New England hills. . . ." But there is, he points out, a further and even more significant point of identity. As a result of reading the Bible Crusoe experienced a deep evangelical experience which opened up to him a strange new world and transformed his life. The Bible, John Mackay points out, has, in like manner, been a supreme fertilizing influence in the development of North American civilization. "What is best in North American life," he boldly affirms, "the precious ore amid much dross, we owe to the heritage that came to us, not from books in general, but from a Book, and from the spiritual awakenings produced by the Book upon innumerable spiritual children of Robinson Crusoe."[1]

[1] *Heritage and Destiny* (S. C. M., London, 1943), p. 86.

147

If the history of Robinson Crusoe is, in this way, "profoundly symbolical," it may be helpful to recapitulate the stages by which, in Defoe's classic, Crusoe came to an understanding of saving faith and an experience of salvation.

Crusoe was grievously sick of a tropical fever and at the point of death when he had a dreadful dream:

> The ague again so violent that I lay a-bed all day, and neither ate nor drank. I was ready to perish for thirst; but so weak, I had not strength to stand up, or to get myself any water to drink. Prayed to God again, but was light-headed; and when I was not, I was so ignorant that I knew not what to say: only lay and cried, Lord, look upon me! Lord, pity me! Lord, have mercy upon me! I suppose I did nothing else for two or three hours; till the fit wearing off, I fell asleep, and did not wake till far in the night. When I awoke, I found myself much refreshed, but weak, and exceedingly thirsty: however, as I had no water in my whole habitation, I was forced to lie till morning, and went to sleep again. In this second sleep I had this terrible dream: I thought that I was sitting on the ground, on the outside of my wall, where I sat when the storm blew after the earthquake, and that I saw a man descend from a great black cloud, in a bright flame of fire, and light upon the ground: he was all over as bright as a flame, so that I could but just bear to look towards him: his countenance was inexpressibly dreadful, impossible for words to describe: when he stepped upon the ground with his feet, I thought the earth trembled, just as it had done before in the earthquake; and all the air looked, to my apprehension, as if it had been filled with flashes of fire. He had no sooner landed upon the earth, but he moved forward towards me, with a long spear or weapon in his hand, to kill me; and when he came to a rising ground, at some distance, he spoke to me, or I heard a voice so terrible that it is impossible to express the terror of it; all that I can say I understood, was this! Seeing all these things have not brought thee to repentance, now thou shalt die; at which words, I thought he lifted up the spear that was in his hand, to kill me.[2]

2 *The Life and Strange Surprising Adventures of Robinson Crusoe of Yorks, Mariner* (Penguin, Harmondsworth, Middx., 1938), Vol. I, p. 125.

Crusoe realized the spiritual peril he was in: he admitted that
he had "lived without desire of good or consciousness of evil";
that he had neither feared God in danger nor been thankful to
Him in deliverance. In his grievous need there was no one
to whom he could turn for assistance or comfort or advice. He
urgently cried to God: "Lord, be my help, for I am in great
distress." "This," he notes, "was the first prayer, if I may
call it so, that I had made for many years."

Crusoe, however, was still ignorant of the meaning of faith.
In his extremity he began to reproach God. What had he
done to deserve such misery? His querulous complaints were
quickly silenced by the accusations of a newly awakened conscience.

> My conscience presently checked me in that inquiry, as if I
> had blasphemed: and methought it spoke to me like a voice!
> Wretch, dost *thou* ask what thou hast done? Look back
> upon a dreadful misspent life, and ask thyself what thou
> hast *not* done? Ask why is it that thou wert not long ago
> destroyed? Why wert thou not drowned in Yarmouth Roads;
> killed in the fight when the ship was taken by the Sallee
> man-of-war; devoured by the wild beasts on the coast of
> Africa; or drowned *here,* when all the crew perished but
> thyself? Dost *thou* ask what thou hast done?[3]

A little later, while searching in an old sea chest for some
tobacco to cure his fever, he found a Bible. Reading the
Scripture he came across the words: "He is exalted a Prince
and a Saviour; to give repentance and to give remission."

> I threw down the book; and with my heart as well as my
> hands lifted up to heaven, in a kind of ecstasy of joy, I
> cried out aloud, Jesus, thou son of David! Jesus, thou
> exalted Prince and Saviour! give me repentance! This
> was the first time in all my life I could say, in the true sense
> of the words, that I prayed; for now I prayed with a sense
> of my condition, and with a true scripture view of hope,
> founded on the encouragement of the word of God: and
> from this time, I may say, I began to have hope that God
> would hear me.[4]

[3] *Ibid.,* p. 132.
[4] *Ibid.,* p. 137.

The consequences of his prayer were a newly found joy, a sense of happy liberation, a consciousness of forgiveness. Crusoe, commenting on this transformation wrought by faith, sententiously observes:

> As for my solitary life, it was nothing; I did not so much as pray to be delivered from it, or think of it; it was all of no consideration, in comparison with this. And I add this part here, to hint to whoever shall read it, that whenever they come to a true sense of things, they will find deliverance from sin a much greater blessing than deliverance from affliction.[5]

These words bear on them the hallmark of authenticity. We may infer that Defoe had himself known a genuine spiritual experience even though (in the opinion of a recent biographer) "over and over again his private life lapsed distressingly from the standards he preached."[6] The words attributed to Crusoe, however, echo, in their faith and fervor, the traditional language of evangelical experience. If John Mackay is right, we, who bear the mark of Cain, need to appropriate, as Crusoe did, the benefits of an accomplished redemption to end alienation and to win acceptance.

[5] *Ibid.*, p. 138.
[6] William Freeman, *The Incredible De Foe* (Herbert Jenkins, London, 1950), p. 294.

General Index

Index of Persons

Abel, 9f.
Acton, Lord, 127
Adam, 9f., 55
Alexander, Lloyd, 43n.
Anderson, Hans, 84
Anselm, 112
Aristophanes, 100
Arnold, Matthew, 98n.
Arnold, Dr. Thomas, 23f.
Auden, W. H., 46
Augustine, 37f., 112, 114

Bach, 112
Bainton, R H., 128n.
Baker, A. E., 89, 134n.
Ballantyne, R. M., 25
Barrett, William, 86, 89n.
Bate, W. J., 93n.
Baudelaire, 28
Bergson, Henri, 39
Bernard of Clairvaux, 127
Bonhoeffer, Dietrich, 94
Booth, William, 102
Boswell, James, 36f., 67, 90n., 92n.
Bray, Billy, 106
Brod, Max, 46n., 52
Browne, Sir Thomas, 132
Browning, Robert, 10

Brunner, Emil, 92
Bunyan, John, 93, 102
Burkitt, E. C., 111n.
Butler, Samuel, 127
Butterfield, Herbert, 116

Cain, 9f., 15, 40, 46f., 150
Calvin, 128
Camus, Albert, 48, 56, 60
Carlyle, Thomas, 82, 121
Cattermole, George, 82
Chadwick, Constance, 104
Charles, King, 95
Chesterton, G. K., 132
Cicero, 98, 100
Clough, 24
Cocks, H. P. Lovell, 80n.
Colton, Charles, 35
Constantine, 127
Coward, Noel, 80
Cowper, William, 65
Crabtree, A. B., 12n.
Cranston, Maurice, 43
Crawshaw, Richard, 110

Dante, 46
Davidman, Joy, 84n.
Defoe, Daniel, 147
Denney, James, 122
Dickens, Charles, 82

Dickenson, G. Lowes, 99
Donne, John, 94
Dostoevsky, Fydor, 14, 18f., 30f., 42, 67, 77, 87f., 117f.
Dryden, 91
Dyson, A. E., 24

Eadmen, 112
Eliot, T. S., 14f., 44, 69n., 74, 91, 96
Epictetus, 97
Epicurus, 90, 99
Euripides, 98
Eve, 9f.

Faraday, Michael, 139
Farmer, Dr., 103
Faulkner, William, 40, 75f.
Feldman, Gene, 139n.
Forsyth, P. T., 14, 77
Fox, J., 95n.
Francis of Assisi, 110f., 130f.
Freeman, William, 150n.
Freud, 138
Frye, Roland Mushat, 68

Gairdner, Temple, 106
Gartenberg, Max, 139n.
Gibbon, 116
Glover, T. R., 97n.
Goethe, 46

155